THE LAST OF THE WHALING CAPTAINS

To my Wife Muriel,
who helped me greatly in the
production of this book.

CAPTAIN MURRAY in Arctic Gear

THE
LAST OF THE
WHALING CAPTAINS

By Captain G. V. CLARK

GLASGOW
BROWN, SON & FERGUSON, LTD.
4-10 DARNLEY STREET

First Edition – 1986

ISBN 0 85174 498 2

FOREWORD

IT is only by chance that the story of Captain John Murray ever came to be recorded. I was home on leave from ships trading permanently in the East and knowing that the number of men who had served in sailing ships was growing steadily less decided to do what I could to obtain the stories of some of them while there was still time. From Captain John Pearson of Tayport, Fife, I got a wonderful account of his time in a wooden emigrant ship to Australia, Arctic whalers and other sailing ships and having given it to me he said: " Captain John Murray is a man you should see—he spent most of his sea life in whalers", and it was through him that I was able to meet Captain Murray.

I found him very willing to talk and sitting there in his house at Wormit, in the shadow of the Forth Bridge, he gave me an account of his life and in addition the loan of various documents, so that the book I eventually wrote is a combination of what he told me and, to a small extent, his own notes. It might have helped if I'd had a tape recorder, but if they were in production at that time (1950) I knew nothing about them. Time was not on my side for my leave was nearly finished, so that the account I got was of necessity not as full as it should have been and, as I found out later, I missed out many points. I met Mrs. Murray and found her a charming woman, but have no knowledge of when they were married—Captain Murray did not mention it. One slight clue only have I got: he was still a batchelor when he took on the establishing of the post on Southampton Island in 1900, when he was 32. He was three years there so was at least 35 when he married. There were two children, boys, one of whom went to sea.

My recollection of Captain Murray is of a tall, lean man with a limp, and I formed the opinion that the Arctic was his real home. Few men would, from choice, have done three years without a break on Southampton Island and yet one is left with the feeling that it was no penance for him. He seemed to almost welcome extreme hardship as something to be fought and defeated. He was a great hunter as is shown by the fact that in September/ October 1900 he shot enough ptarmigan to last the settlement all the winter, and there were at least one hundred people there. His remark that he thought his tally of 103 polar bears shot with his own rifle is a record is probably correct and might have found a place in the "Guinness Book of Records". But as any claim has to be covered by clear proof of accuracy, which would be impossible, Captain Murray's achievement must remain unrecorded. Any such record as the above would not be welcomed today, for the uncontrolled killing of polar bears resulted, quite inevitably, in its near-extinction and today they are a protected species and on the increase.

I am thankful that I knew Captain Murray, for he was one of the last men living who had crossed the North Atlantic in small wooden square-riggers and groped his way round Hudson's Bay in them without benefit of an engine. He apparently thought nothing at all of all he had done, which fits in with the fact that he was the most modest man I have known.

CONTENTS

ILLUSTRATIONS

xi

CHAPTER ONE

FIRST VOYAGE

ON 8th June, 1914 the steam whaling barques *Active*, Captain John Murray, and *Morning*, Captain James Fairweather, left Dundee on what was to be the very last venture employing vessels of their type ever to leave Britain. Captain Fairweather died in March 1933, leaving Captain Murray as the last of the old-time whaling masters in Britain.

Captain John Murray was born at Peterhead on 26th July, 1868. He came of a sea-faring stock, which is hardly surprising in Peterhead, where there must be few people who could not find sea-farers among their forebears. His father, a whaling master, had been in the *Felix* with Ross in his search for traces of Sir John Franklin's ill-fated expedition and received an Arctic medal for his services. He was later in command of the whaler *Windward* for eight years, among other vessels.

Born in Peterhead and the son of a whaling master, it was almost inevitable that John Murray should have chosen to go to sea. It seems certain that just as some people may be a born surgeon or teacher or artist or engineer, so was John Murray a born seaman. In the spring of 1883, when he was fourteen, he, together with another boy, stowed away aboard his father's ship, the *Windward*,shortly before she set off on her annual whaling voyage. The first attempt to go to sea did not succeed, however, for the two lads were discovered hiding under an upturned boat, hauled out and put ashore. But the following year, 1884, his father allowed him to go and he shipped aboard the *Windward* as an Ordinary Seaman.

1884 was the year in which the first systematic examination of the weather in Hudson's Bay, an area which Captain Murray was to know so well for nearly fifty years, was carried out. In

July of that year the well-known Newfoundland sealer *Neptune* set off from Halifax N.S. under the command of Lt. A. R. Gordon, having on board a number of meteorologists who were left at various points to spend the winter there and study climatic conditions. There were five of these bases and each one was given the name of the meteorologist in charge. Thus we have Port Burwell, just inside Cape Chudleigh; Ashe Inlet, on the north side of Hudson Strait; Stupart's Bay, opposite to it on the south side; Port de Boucherville on Nottingham Island, and Port Laperriere, on the western side of the two Digges Islands.

The *Windward* had been built at Peterhead in 1860 as a sailing vessel, barque rigged, but the days of the sailing whaler, in Britain at least but certainly not in the U.S.A., were nearly finished even when she was built and she had engines installed at Aberdeen in 1866. They were of no great power, only 30 H.P., but were to prove invaluable to her on countless occasions. When seen on a photograph, usually in an Arctic setting, with no other object to give a comparison of their real size, the whalers look quite large, but were in actual fact tiny vessels by modern standards. The *Windward* was only 321 gross tons, 246 nett, 118 feet long by 29 feet beam and 17 feet depth, a proportion of about four beams to length, which made her a tubby little ship. (As a comparison, the tea clipper *Cutty Sark*, still with us, has a proportion of about six beams to length). Like the majority of the Scottish whalers the *Windward* had single topsails fitted with Cunningham's patent reefing gear, a design which was not unlike a venetian blind, the yard actually revolving and rolling the sail with it to reduce or increase its area. She also had a bentinck boom on her foresail, another fitting seen on practically all the whalers and on the Geordie collier brigs. This boom was laced on the foot of the fore course, with a central "tack" on which the boom pivoted, tacks and sheets being secured to the ends of it for handling.

It was about the 1st March 1884 that the *Windward* with young Murray aboard her on his first voyage sailed from Peterhead for the Greenland Sea whale fishery, the whalers *Germanica* (schooner), *Eclipse* (ship), *Hope* (ship), *Erik* (ship),

Earl of Mar & Kellie (barque), *Perseverance* (barque), *Catherine* (snow) and *Alert* (brig) also going to the Greenland Sea this year from Peterhead. From Dundee sixteen whalers went to the north after seals and whales.

Sailing day for the Scottish whalers was a somewhat hectic affair due to the fact that it was preceded, the evening before, by the Sailors' Foy. This was a party, usually held in a public house, attended by the wives and sweethearts and friends of the men who were setting off in the morning for "the fishing". Strong drink played a not inconspicuous part in the evening's entertainment and as the night advanced, proceedings inevitably became somewhat riotous, with fights not unknown. The police kept away on Foy Night as much as possible. The next morning there were plenty of sore heads, but the man who did not have a bottle of whiskey (it was three shillings and sixpence in those days)to share with his friends on sailing day was hardly worth the name of whaler, and it was often something of a job to get the ship unmoored. Even men who normally did not drink regarded sailing day as the one occasion when they could relax a little. The day was a big one for the children, too, for it was usual to give them a holiday to see the ships depart on their venture. It was often a venture in the literal sense, for it was customary for people to buy shares in a voyage and receive a pro rata return of whatever profits the ship made.

At last the moorings were singled up, the inevitable stragglers were helped aboard by their friends, the tug took the weight of the tow rope and the *Windward* moved away from the quay. Once outside the dock, all hands were called aft to give three cheers in reply to a farewell from the shore, but in view of the state of many of the crew it was a somewhat ragged performance. The tug stood by to help them over the bar as there was a heavy swell running outside, and was then cast off and given three cheers as the *Windward* rang full ahead on her engines—six knots!—and set off on her voyage. It was not long before the barque felt the swell and started labouring heavily and soon the young sailor's romantic ideas about life afloat were swept away by the miseries of sea-sickness. One of the sailors took pity on him and advised him to stay on deck and eat some hard tack (ship's biscuit). The first part of the advice, at least, was good, for the air in the small focsle, crowded with men, many of them drunk or half-drunk and smoking shag tobacco, was enough to turn any but the strongest of stomachs. The first bout of sea-sickness was soon over, for within a day or two the *Windward* had arrived in Lerwick to pick up extra men as boat-steerers, harpooners and seamen, as the Shetland Islanders had a fine reputation as seamen, particularly for boat work. As soon as the men had finished work for the day, many of them went ashore, ostensibly to buy the famous Shetland shawls for their wives and sweethearts. Tait was the shipchandler in Lerwick and it was he who arranged for the men, who were mostly without money. Good as their intentions may have been, there must have been many wives who did not receive their Shetland shawls, for no sooner were they ashore when most of the men made for a small public house near the wharf to find a cure for their still aching heads.

After a stay of some days the *Windward* left Lerwick for the whaling grounds. The windlass, one of the type fitted with levers working up and down, was manned and to the tune of "Fare you well my pretty young girl, we're bound for the Rio Grande" the anchor was hove up. The fact that they were bound in the opposite direction to the Rio Grande, to the Greenland Sea, made no difference to the heartiness with which the chanty was sung. Once clear of the harbour the barque soon felt the westerly swell and for about a week young Murray was completely helpless with sea-sickness. The doctor gave him some "medicine" and when he brought up what looked like blood he was somewhat alarmed until he found it was claret the doctor had given him. If he could have got ashore then, he would never have set foot on board a ship again, as he told the writer more than sixty years later.

As they got into the ice they came across seals and shot them whenever possible. The first one shot, the dinghy was lowered to pick it up and young Murray, his sea-sickness gone by now, for the ice had smoothed the sea, was first into the boat but was soon told by another Ordinary Seaman, who had made one previous voyage to Greenland, to get out "as only experienced men were allowed to do that work". Being now in waters where whales might be expected, the crow's nest was rigged and the boats, six of them, were swung out, each having five whale lines of 120 fathoms each (three quarters of a mile of line), and carrying six men: harpooner in charge, boat steerer and four oarsmen. Three watches were set: mate, second mate and spectioneer, each having a harpooner on watch with him, one being on the bridge, the other in the crow's nest on the lookout for whales. The harpooner was the one who killed the whale and naturally an important man on a whaler, on whose skill the whole success of the voyage could depend, and as such was classed as an officer. According to Albert Hastings Markham in his book "A Whaling Cruise to Baffin's Bay" the spectioneer was "the officer under whose direction the whale is cut up" and he tells us the name is derived from the Dutch "spek" meaning blubber. In Lindsay's book "A Voyage to the Arctic in the whaler *Aurora*" he defines the spectioneer as the "chief of the harpooners", while Barron's "Old Whaling Days" gives the spectioneer as "the chief harpooner who directs the cutting operations of stripping the whale of its blubber" and also states that it is an old Dutch word. Constantly in whaling terminology one comes across words which have a Dutch origin, showing the extent to which the Dutch participated in and dominated the whaling industry in earlier days.

As this account of Captain Murray's career deals almost entirely with whales and whaling, it is necessary to mention the types of whales for which the *Windward* was searching. Incidentally, in whaling parlance a whale was never referred to as such but as a "fish" in spite of the fact that it is not a fish but a mammal. There were five species: the right (sometimes called bowhead), the finback or rorqual, the bottlenose, the white and the narwhal. The sperm whale or cachalot was never mentioned by Captain Murray and he certainly never caught one. The right whale was the most highly prized, because of the large amount of bone and blubber it had, but even when John Murray first went to the whaling in 1884 this whale had been nearly exterminated and he told me that he never killed a right whale or a finback. As regards the origin of the name right whale it was so-called because it was the right whale to go for, because of its value. In the year John Murray went to sea whale oil was £33 a ton and whale bone £1150 a ton. A whale would often give a ton or more of bone so it can be seen that even one could go some way towards paying the costs of a whaling voyage. The bone referred to was not really bone as generally understood, being a curtain of horney substance suspended from the palate designed to act as a strainer for the whale's food, which is a minute organism known as krill, a shrimplike species.

The finback, or finner, which attains a length of about 80 feet was in those days left alone by Scottish whalers. As one writer observed: "they have little oil and short bone so are not pursued. They are also very quick in their movements and consequently dangerous". Another writer remarks: "This whale is accounted almost worthless by the whalers and on account of the small quantity of oil which it yields and the difficulty of its capture, it is never attacked unless by mistake or through ignorance.

1868 may be taken as the year in which modern whale catching started, and it is truly remarkable that the old style of whaling was practised for many years after that date. Not only was it practised but the old type of whaler, which was extremely costly to build, was still produced right up into the 1880's. It is an example of the conservatism of British whaling ideas that this was allowed to happen and Captain Murray never ceased to stress that this conservatism or reluctance to change was the real cause of the decline of Scottish whaling. Regarding the finner whales, Charles Edward, writing in 1868, says: "They are never meddled with as they yield but a small quantity of blubber and, besides, are very tenacious of life". But he adds that "an American vessel comes every year to the neighbourhood of Iceland in pursuit of these whales, which are killed by firing both harpoon and rocket into them simultaneously"—another example of the initiative lacking in British whalers.

These statements were made in the 1870's and yet, even before then, a Norwegian had perfected a system which was to alter the whole technique of whale killing. His name was Svend Foyn, born at Tonsberg in 1809, and in his early years

he confined his activities to seal-hunting. But as time went by
he conceived the idea that the great rorquals, the finners, the
"fish" few dared to tackle because of their great size and
strength, were the species which could make whaling into an
industry instead of a risky venture. He invented the modern
harpoon gun and built a ship to carry it in. He called her the
Spes et Fides and she was the prototype of the modern whale
catcher.

The species most frequently encountered in the Arctic, if one
excludes the white whale, is the bottle-nosed whale, which
runs to about thirty feet in length for the male, twenty-four for
the females. It does not have the curtain of bone which made
the right whale so valuable but was hunted for its blubber and
the valuable spermacete, somewhat similar to that found in
the sperm whale or cachalot. These whales are migratory and
are not infrequently stranded on the coasts of the U.K. In his
book "Modern Whaling and Bear Hunting" W. G. Burn
Murdoch has said: "Curiously, there have been more lives lost
at bottlenose whaling than at that of the larger kinds". The
white whale or beluga was hunted for its blubber and its skin,
which was used for making boots and was generally called, for
some reason, "porpoise hide". It attains a length of about
fifteen feet and generally travels in herds, the method of
capture being to drive them into shallow water and either net
them or kill them by shooting or harpooning. When under
water, white whales make a peculiar whistling sound and
because of this were called by the whalers "sea canaries". It
took about six of them to produce a ton of oil.

The narwhal, last of the whale species, is really a cousin of
the white whale. It has a tusk growing out of one side of its
upper jaw, usually the left, which sometimes reaches a length
of eight or nine feet or even more and this has given it the
name of unicorn among whalers, shortened to "unie". Its
value lay in its ivory tusk and the good quality of the oil
obtained from it: about four narwhals produce a ton of oil. In
the 1860's narwhal horn was from 24/- to 30/- a pound
weight and a single horn would weigh twenty pounds or more.
The Chinese used to have a high regard for the tusk of the
narwhal, from a medicinal point of view, believing it to have

aphrodisiacal qualities. In J. C. Well's book "The Gateway to the Polynia" he describes a use to which the carcass of the narwhal was put: after disembowelling, the carcass was placed back to wind and the interior stuffed with wood and oakum and set alight. The smell from the burning flesh would travel for miles and attract polar bears, who apparently found it irresistible. Of all the species hunted by man in the Arctic, the narwhal was the most difficult to kill. It would not stay still for long and would never let one get close to it, and very little of it ever showed above water to give one the chance of a shot at it. The instant it was hit by a harpoon it would dive steeply down, in the same manner as the Greenland right whale, but would soon return to the surface, where it could be lanced. More than one writer has told us of the vast number of narwhals they saw in the Arctic: Charles Edward Smith in "From the Deep of the Sea" remarks that "many thousands of narwhales (sic) have been passing the ship today, all heading up the Sound (Lancaster Sound) in little companies. The captain tells me they always make their appearance here at this time of year (July 1st) and are sure indicators of the presence of whales, which appear immediately after the narwhales". That was in 1866, only 18 years before John Murray first went to the Arctic. J. C. Wells in "The Gateway to the Polynia" tells us that "we saw them going in flocks of many thousands, travelling north in their migrations, tusk to tusk and tail to tail, like a regiment of cavalry...". Wells was a passenger in the schooner yacht *Sampson* in 1872 when he wrote the above. But in little more than a decade later such spectacles were already a thing of the past and as this account will show, the years immediately before John Murray went to sea, saw an end of "the good old days of whaling". The Polynia used in the title of Wells' book, means a space of open water in a mass of ice.

As regards the method of killing the whales, in Scottish vessels a gun fitted in the bows of the boat and firing a non-explosive harpoon was used and a darting gun, propelled by hand was also used at times. When the harpoon had penetrated a certain distance into the whale, an iron rod came into contact with the skin and actuated a trigger which exploded a bomb lance into the whale. This latter was originally an American idea, and Captain Murray frequently remarked that he regarded American methods of killing whales as superior to the Scottish. Sometimes a rocket was fired into the whale from a harpoon gun, and Lindsay in his book "A Voyage to the Arctic in the Whaler Aurora" mentions a "Welsh's rocket" being used. Immediately after being harpooned the whale would dive, sometimes to a depth of 200 fathoms or more and this was the moment of greatest danger for the boat's crew, for the line would go flying out at a great rate and take anything with it which fouled it. Many men lost their lives in this way. The completely different techniques of Scottish and American whaling will be referred to later, but as regards the actual killing of the whales it may be mentioned that American boats were fitted with a centre board and sailed right up to a whale, while Scottish boats had no centre board and pulled up to their quarry. There seems no doubt that American boats were far superior to British.

In the Scottish whalers, in the old days, the 1st May was the traditional date for the initiation of all first voyagers to the Arctic into the circle of true whalers, and the ceremony was duly carried out aboard the *Windward*. In the first dog watch(4 to 6 p.m.) those who had not been in the Arctic before were led forward and put down on top of the coal in the tiny forepeak, and the hatch shut down on them. The doctor carried by all whalers was one of the initiates but could not be found for some time. When run to earth in his bunk he appealed to the captain to be omitted from the ceremony but his appeal was rejected and he joined the others down the peak. The ceremony was almost identical with the oft-described one of Crossing the Line and was carried out in the tweendecks, the only omission being the part where the neophyte was dumped into a bath of water at the end. The novices were blindfolded and led into the tweendecks one at a time, held firmly and "soaped" with a mixture of Archangel tar, soot and molasses which was then shaved off with a razor made from a piece of hoop iron. Various ridiculous questions were asked of them and when any of the initiates unthinkingly opened their mouth to attempt to answer, the "shaving brush" was promptly pushed into it. The doctor took it badly and was somewhat roughly handled, his rubber collar, the only one he possessed, being ruined. After all initiates had been dealt with, the "foo-foo" band marched round the decks, playing on various instruments including some of the cook's pots and pans and were rewarded with a generous tot of rum, after which a sing-song was held in the focsle.

The ceremony aboard the *Windward* in 1884 appears to have been the same as that referred to by A. H. Markham in his book "A Whaling Cruise to Baffin's Bay", with one difference. Writing aboard the Dundee whaler in 1873 he says: "Saturday May 31st: today we crossed the Arctic Circle. Formerly it was customary on board whale ships to perform a ceremony somewhat similar to that still in vogue on board most men-of-war and other ships when crossing the equator. Since the introduction of steamers into this trade, the practise, like many others, has gone completely out of fashion". The only difference between Captain Murray's account of initiation into the Arctic brotherwood and Markham's version being that the former gives 1st May as the fixed date for it while the latter says it took place when crossing the Arctic Circle. Barron's "Old Whaling Days" gives the same version as Captain Murray, also mentioning a garland being hung from the main topgallant stay.

Life in the Scottish whalers was completely different to that aboard an ordinary merchant ship, in some ways harder and in others very much easier. The little *Windward* had a crew of more than fifty men and, with four quartermasters to attend to the steering, the majority of the crew had that much-prized privilege of "all night in". As regards food, the men were issued monthly with certain dry stores such as tea, coffee beans, brown sugar, butter, jam, marmalade, limejuice, canned meat, and cooked their breakfast and evening meals, the cook preparing only the midday meal. Thursday and Sunday were the traditional days for duff, good solid stuff about which it used to be jokingly said that anyone falling overboard just after eating it would sink like a stone.

Despite the wintery conditions which they were certain to encounter, the crew of a Scottish whaler had to provide all their own clothes. The regulars, who went in the whalers every year, invariably had fine outfits, often made for them by the Eskimos, but the casuals who sometimes made up the crews were in some cases very poorly fitted out. The wages were the usual ones prevailing in a port before the days of wage standardisation but they received a share of any profits made on the voyage, although these were very often negligible if the voyage was a poor one. Practically all the men in the whalers were from the ship's home port of Peterhead or Dundee, and this fact led to a good relationship between all hands, very different to the conditions aboard some American whalers. As an example of the different type of discipline in Scottish whalers, Commander A. H. Markham in his book "A Whaling Cruise to Baffin's Bay" Tells us that aboard the *Arctic* "everybody was called by his christian name, a habit I soon adopted". This, coming from a naval officer, is rather remarkable when one thinks of the discipline under which Markham had been brought up.

John Murray's first voyage to sea in the *Windward* was not a particularly successful one for the owners. The total catch was one right whale, a few bottlenose and a fair number of sealskins. They had bad luck with one right whale, for after getting fast, the line parted and the fish got away, but was picked up dead later by another ship which claimed it as its own. One boat's crew had a narrow escape, illustrating the risky nature of a whaler's life. A bottlenose whale was harpooned but when it dived the line became fouled and the boat was dragged half under water before the line parted. There were no casualties beyond a wetting in the icy water for the boat's crew. Polar bears were very frequently seen on these whaling voyages and it was a Peterhead rule, but not a Dundee one, that the skins of any bears shot were the captain's property. On this voyage in the *Windward* the barque was lying one evening moored up to an ice floe when two bears were seen in the distance. The cook immediately got busy stoking his galley fire with bones and the smell soon attracted the bears. When they approached, the larger one was shot and killed but the other made off at great pace. It was cornered in a pool on an ice floe until one of the harpooners arrived with a rifle and shot it. On another occasion on this voyage one of the boats encountered a mother bear and cub swimming. The cub was lassooed and hauled close to the boat, upon which the mother attacked the boat and tried to climb in, nearly upsetting it before the harpooner shot it. A cruel and merciless business, the Arctic hunting.

"WINDWARD"

Having little success at the whaling, the *Windward* sailed westward towards the coast of Greenland in search of bladder-nose or hooded seals, so called because of the large inflatable sac on the nose of the male. A hooded seal can be a nasty customer when wounded, as one of the *Windward's* men found. Having been left on the ice to flench (skin) several seals which had been shot, this man was chased by a wounded seal which grabbed him by the seat of his trousers and hung on until his yells scared it sufficiently to cause it to let go and allow him to escape.

This voyage lasted only about six months and the *Windward* was back in Peterhead in August 1884. It was unusual for a whaler to return to her home port in the summer and Captain Barron, writing in 1895, says: ''....the crews of these whalers and sealers were at home only during the winter months and not, in fact, the whole of these, as they commenced their voyages usually in February or early in March. The result was in my own case (seeing that I did not miss a year for the seal or whale fisheries for a full seventeen years) that during this long period I never saw either blossom or fruit upon the trees, and my eyes and senses were not blessed with the scent of growing flowers, the sight of ripening corn or the subsequent harvest operations. On the contrary, my most constant surroundings during these years were ice, snow, fogs or the boundless expanse of ocean''.*

John Murray left the *Windward* at the end of this voyage but the vessel was to have many more adventures before she finished. He told me he was the only man who could, offhand, give her subsequent history. Some time after he left her she was sold to Captain Wiggins, whose name is associated with the Kara Sea, for work in that area, a man called Frederick C. Jackson being in her during that period. She changed owners again after that, being bought by Alfred Harmsworth, later Lord Northcliffe, well known publisher, who, together with Jackson financed the Jackson Harmsworth Expedition of 1894/96. It was this expedition which met Fridtjof Nansen in June 1896 after his truly remarkable journey with one companion, Lieutenant Hjolmar Johannesen in an attempt to reach the North Pole. The attempt failed and the two men reached the Jackson Harmsworth Expedition at a point in Franz Josef Land after being alone together with no other human contact from 14th March, 1895 to 17th June, 1896. They were taken back to Norway in the *Windward*. John Murray later saw his old ship in the South-west India dock in London where she was being completely overhauled, having been presented to Admiral Peary by Alfred Harmsworth for an attempt to reach the North Pole. This was in 1898 and the old ship had as her commander Captain John Bartlett, uncle of the famous Newfoundland seafarer Captain Bob Bartlett. The latter was mate of the *Windward* for four years and then carried on with Peary, for whom he had a great admiration, when he got the *Roosevelt*, a

* ''Old Whaling Days'' by Captain William Barron.

ship specially built for Arctic work and which replaced the *Windward*. Her work with Peary finished, the *Windward* went back to Scotland in 1904 as a whaler, but with Dundee on her stern instead of Peterhead. The Arctic claimed her eventually, for she was wrecked in Davis Straits on June 25th, 1907, two of her crew dying of exposure later. Lloyds' Register for 1907/08 gives the master's name as J.J. Cooney. She was 47 years old when wrecked.

CHAPTER TWO

FIRST WINTER IN THE ARCTIC

FROM the *Windward* Captain Murray went to the whaling barque *Perseverance* and in 1885 we find his son shipping aboard the vessel as an Ordinary Seaman. His wages were thirty shillings a month and he signed on for a voyage which promised to extend well over a year, as it was intended that the vessel should winter in the Arctic. The idea behind this being that she would be on the spot ready for the whales at the break-up of the ice the following spring. Although his father was master of the barque John Murray received no preferential treatment and had to find his own way if he wanted a berth. He and a friend went down aboard the *Perseverance* looking for a job and found the mate superintending the sending aloft of the upper yards, and in none too sweet a temper. In answer to their question as to whether he had engaged all his men he growled out: "What the hell's it got to do with you, anyhow?" but relaxed a bit later and the friend got an AB's job while John was taken on as an Ordinary Seaman. They worked by the ship for some days before sailing, getting sails, stores, whale-lines and other whaling gear down to the boil yard from the warehouse in which they had been stored during the winter. The boil house was the place where the blubber brought home by the whalers was boiled down into oil, and between it and the warehouse was a snug little pub. For some of those engaged in bringing down the equipment from the warehouse, this was too much of a temptation and as Captain Murray told me, they were a happy crowd to start with and got happier as the day advanced, for it was two drinks per trip, one up and one down, toasting the success of the coming voyage.

At last all the stores were aboard, sails bent and the crew signed on. One of the seamen, an Irishman, was unable to give a home address when being signed on and the captain jokingly said to the Shipping Master: "Just put down the police station, for he spends most of his time ashore there!" to which Pat replied: "The address will find me alright, sorr, but me discharges are good!".

Following the signing-on was the Foy Night and as a result there were a number of thick heads when the men joined the next morning to take her away to sea. It happened to be a Friday and Old Tom, the veteran of the focsle, was loud in his condemnation of sailing on such a day. He couldn't see "how the hell the owners expected any luck, sailing on a Friday", but Old Tom couldn't see much anyhow, for the Foy Night had left him with two lovely black eyes! The men were sitting there in the tiny focsle, some of them half drunk, when the mate shouted down the scuttle the good news that the captain had decided not to sail until the next day, perhaps in deference to the old superstition about sailing on a Friday. The news brought general rejoicing and after "giving her a jig at the pump" until they got a suck, the crew was allowed to go home, to rejoin the next morning.

There was a big crowd of wives, sweethearts, friends and schoolchildren to see them off the next day, the latter no doubt hoping to see one or two take a very cold bath as they tried to get aboard and toppled into the dock, as sometimes happened. At last the mate had got all his men aboard and the *Perseverance* left the dockside. Passing the pierhead the customary three cheers were given by those ashore and replied to as best as they could by the ship's crew and the barque sailed. And sailing aboard the *Perseverance* was really sailing and not the meaningless expression it had become in a vessel fitted with engines, for where in the *Windward* they got headway and manoeuvrability on her by ringing a telegraph and getting the use of the engines, in the *Perseverance* any progress they made depended on sails alone, as the barque had no engines and was a pure sailing vessel. Consequently, they had to start getting sail on her as soon as they had left the dock. Like the *Windward* the *Perseverance* had single topsails and Cunningham's patent reefing gear for them and there were scenes of great activity and no doubt some profanity while the sails were being set. The chantyman Andy was called for and the topsails crept up the masts to the strains of "Blow the man down"—truly a scene from the past, with the tiny barque with her single topsails leaving the little grey town for the Arctic seas. And tiny the *Perseverance* was, for she had a gross tonnage of only 179, which in spite of her two square-rigged masts made her no bigger than a coasting schooner. Her dimensions were 101 × 23 × 13, giving her a beams to length proportion of 4·4. She had been built at Newcastle in 1852 so was already over thirty years old when John Murray sailed in her. She was not the first whaler of this name, for in the book "From the Deep of the Sea" a *Perseverance* is mentioned by Captain Gravill of the whaler *Diana*. He tells us that in 1818 he was an officer in the *Cherub* of Hull and met "the old *Perseverance*" up in North Greenland. But the name has always been a favourite one for ships and the Lloyd's Register for 1878 has sixteen vessels so named, all but one being sailing ships.

When well clear of the bar the tug was cast off and the *Perseverance* set off with a light favourable wind. It was fortunate that the wind was fair and the weather was good, for there were few aboard in a condition to be of much use in an emergency. Such an emergency had occurred only two years earlier, in 1883, when the Dundee steam whaling barque *Mazinthien* was driven ashore at Peterhead in a blizzard soon after leaving Dundee for Davis Straits. The entire crew was rescued by the rocket apparatus but the vessel was a total loss. The iron full rigged ship *Dunstaffnage*, which left Dundee in tow at the same time as the *Mazinthien* was much less lucky, for she disappeared with all hands after her tow rope parted.

Once the strenuous business of getting sail on the barque had been completed most of those who had been capable of working, retired to the focsle for a smoke and a drink—if they had one. Old Tom, waking from a drunken sleep and finding his bottle empty, croaked out: "is there no-one can save a life? Here, Bob, hold yer dam tongue, lying in yer bunk howlin' 'far far frae Bonny Scotland'. What the hell did ye ever leave it for, for it'll be a mighty long time before ye see it again". Some of the men had brought oatmeal puddings, done up in strings, and oatmeal cakes with them, and these had to do for a meal, as both cook and steward were temporarily "indisposed", the former lying dead to the world on a locker in the galley, the steward in the same state in his bunk. Sailing day in the whalers!

The focsle was a crowded little triangle up in the bows, the bunks lining the sides. They were fitted with sliding doors and it was customary for two or three of the men to bunk together. It was a rough life for a boy to enter, but one which quickly sorted out those with a real aptitude from those who had been attracted only by its "romantic" aspects. That evening the watches were picked. This voyage the barque was bound for Cumberland Gulf, off Davis Straits, and not calling at Lerwick for extra men as had been done the previous year in the *Windward*, as it was expected to complete the crew with Eskimos on arrival in the Arctic. For the passage out, therefore, the crew was kept on four on and four off, although with a comparatively large crew this was no great hardship.

The next morning quite a few of the men were feeling sorry for themselves, with aching heads and no "hair of the dog that bit them" to bring any relief. Following a conference abaft the windlass, they all trooped aft, headed by Old Tom, to see the steward, who was in as bad a case as they were. In response to the enquiry as to whether the captain was awake, the steward went and knocked at the captain's door and told him the crew wanted to see him. "They're not feeling well, sir, and want to know if you can cure a headache". The captain replied that as yet the seals had not been broken on the liquor store, but "you'll find a good substitute, steward, in the after locker". The steward took a large jar from the locker and brought it on deck to the waiting men, whose downcast faces lit up when they saw the jar. Old Tom was the first for a drink and eagerly accepted the generous tot handed to him by the steward. His mouth was in such a shocking state that he had swallowed most of it before he realised that it was not the drink he had expected, but he kept a straight face and handed the glass back with "that's good stuff, steward" and the next man stepped forward for his whack. He too played up and so did the others who followed him, until all had a good dose of—black draught.

It soon put them to rights and they enjoyed the joke played on them. The story is recorded here as an illustration of the different conditions prevailing in the whalers to those in an ordinary merchant ship, for aboard one of the latter it would have been unthinkable for the crew to go aft asking for a drink the day after sailing.

Before signing on, young Murray had noticed some of the old hands marking with chalk certain bunks in the focsle. This, it appeared, was an old custom, for having put his mark on what he considered the best situated bunk, a man could claim it for the voyage. John and a friend accordingly selected what they considered a good bunk, but it was not long after sailing that they found that they had made a poor choice, for the deckhead leaked badly, their bedclothes were soaked and they had a miserable time of it.

One night soon after sailing, Old Tom was turning in for his watch below when he sprang out of his bunk cursing and swearing and brandishing what turned out to be a pig's foot. There were various superstitions in the whalers which veterans like Old Tom took very seriously and among them was the one that a pig's foot or tail placed in a whaleboat would bring bad luck to that boat for the whole season. To even mention pig, salmon or hare aboard a whaler was to invite bad luck, and the superstition general in sailing ships regarding whistling when a wind was already blowing, was very strongly felt in the whalers. D. M. Lindsay in "A Voyage to the Arctic in the Whaler *Aurora*" mentions that he shot a hare at St. John's NFL but was not allowed to take it on board, Captain Fairweather stopping him as he stepped on to the gangway. The individual who put the pig's foot in Old Tom's bunk was never found, but as things turned out the superstition regarding a pig's foot had some support this voyage.

Sailing between the Orkneys and Shetlands the *Perseverance* had favourable winds until well over towards Davis Straits, where she encountered a series of heavy north-westerly gales. One night, with the barque hove-to under a goosewinged main topsail, young Murray was sheltering in the lee of a weather cloth in the main rigging and whistling softly to himself when he got a cuff across the ear from Old Tom, also in his watch, who exclaimed: "damn you, don't you have enough wind now, without whistling for more?" Despite the fact that his father was in command, this made no difference to John's position aboard the ship and before ever sailing with his father he was told that whatever he heard for'd he was never to repeat it aft.

Eventually the *Perseverance* passed Cape Farewell, at the southern tip of Greenland, in 60 North, and soon afterwards they sighted their first iceberg. From then onwards they were among the ice the whole time, and having worked across Davis Straits commenced sailing up Cumberland Sound, running before a strong easterly wind. The next morning found the wind increased to a strong gale, blowing right up the Sound. It was what was known to the whalers as a "strong ale wind", for this reason: with such a wind a vessel was in great danger of being blown onto the ice and "nipped". If this happened and she had to be abandoned, it was commonplace for the crew to broach the ship's liquor, rather on the principle of "eat, drink and be merry for tomorrow we die". Captain Barron mentions such an incident in his "Old Whaling Days" when some of the crew of the sunken *Queen Charlotte* got at the liquor and caused a lot of trouble. Unable to find shelter on either side of the Sound, the *Perseverance* was hove-to in a very heavy sea, in itself an extremely dangerous operation due to the risk of capsizing when she got the wind and sea abeam. At daylight next morning they found they were driving in towards the pack and all hands knew they were in a very dangerous position. They were on a dead lee shore, but in a much worse situation than had it been an ordinary rocky coast, for there they would at least have had a chance of saving themselves. But here, once blown onto the edge of the ice, the end would be swift. There have been many examples of the speed with which a whaler would be destroyed by the enormous power of the ice floes. For example, there was the *North Britain* in 1830, when the surgeon, sitting in the cabin, saw both sides of the ship being crushed in towards him and barely had time to get on deck before she sank. The grey dour day, the roar of the gale, the thundering, crashing ice floes, the icy spray sweeping over the tiny vessel, the edge of the pack growing ever closer, were all factors that would have appalled and stampeded into panic any but the truly courageous.

There was only one possible course to take, and quickly, if they were to save the ship, and that was the operation known to whalers as "running the pack", always regarded as a last desperate forlorn hope. It consisted of crowding on all possible sail and steering for the place in the pack which seemed to offer the best chance of working into the ice and thus losing the swell. John's father took this course and going up into the crow's nest gave orders for the helm to be put up. Slowly the *Perseverance* swung round and headed for the pack. All possible sail was put on her and after that it was a case of waiting, seeing her rapidly draw near the pack and wondering what the next few minutes held for them. As Captain Murray told me: "I guess we all had a strange feeling in our stomachs".

In a very short time the barque struck the ice and under the pressure of the sails was forced into the pack about twice her own length. Once in among the ice, the old vessel's strength was tested to the full, the ice floes striking her with such violence as to throw men off their feet, several being injured in this way. The ship's tow-ropes and all the spare timber they had were used as fenders to keep the ice off her sides but were of little value, being ground into a pulp almost at once. As soon as possible, men got down onto the ice and shovelled snow and ice in between the ship and the pack, for the same purpose. One big danger was getting the rudder damaged and to lessen the chances of this happening, it was kept amidships as much as possible. Incidentally, the helmsman's job was sometimes a dangerous one when among the ice, for a bump from a pan on the rudder could send the steering wheel flying round in a violent manner.

Once the vessel had worked her way into a berth in the ice, the immediate danger was reduced (but by no means removed) for the ice lessened the swell as she lay fairly quiet. The opportunity was taken to get some food, for through all the critical moments the cook had kept his galley fire going and had some pea soup ready for the men. But it was not long before there was another cry for all hands on deck. The barque was now being carried along, together with the ice pack, by a strong current which was forcing the whole mass towards a large berg with a projecting point rather like the shear of a plough, and it was obvious that if she were swept onto this projection she would be over in a moment. The boats were swung out almost level with the ice, ready for lowering onto it if the worst happened and food was brought up ready for throwing onto the ice if she foundered. But once again they were lucky, a large piece of floe ice catching on the projecting spear and swinging the vessel clear.

Narrow as her escape had been so far, worse was to come. Having swung clear of the berg, wind and tide were now carrying the imprisoned ship directly towards a group of small islands and reefs about three miles away. She was quite helpless, and with nothing to do but wait events, the captain ordered an issue of rum to the half-frozen, exhausted crew. Soon there was another cry for all hands but this time they were not so fortunate. The barque was swept in between two small inlets and in an attempt to bring her up, both anchors were let go, unavailingly, for a large piece of ice swept across the cables and the vessel dragged stern-first onto one of the islets and was ashore. It was night-time by now, raining heavily, and nothing could be done until daylight when, with a rising tide they managed to get her afloat again. But on the next ebb tide, the forefoot caught on a ledge of rock and as the tide fell further, the stern sank under water and she developed a heavy starboard list. The situation was now desperate and when the ice alongside opened sufficiently for a boat to be put in the water, they set about landing stores and personal belongings, work which was made particularly miserable by very heavy rain. As the tide ebbed, the stern sank deeper and the starboard list got worse, until the water had reached a level where it was nearly up to the entrance to the cabin. Once it was there, the vessel would go quickly down stern first, and Captain Murray gave orders that no-one was to attempt to enter the cabin.

Soundings were taken and it was found that there was twelve feet between the ledge on which the forefoot was caught and the rocky bottom below. It was night-time again by now and with the foolhardiness of youth, John Murray disobeyed his father's order about not entering the poop and, unknown to anyone, worked his way along the port side and entered the cabin. His reason for doing this was to rescue a double-barrelled shotgun which he greatly coveted before the ship went down, as it seemed certain she would do. The interior of the tiny poop was designed with bunks and a table on the port side and the captain's room to starboard, and having reached the poop in the intense darkness, John scrambled into the main cabin. Hanging onto a bunk board on the port side, he estimated that by letting go, he would be able to drop onto the table. Instead, he crashed through the door of the captain's room, nearly horizontal because of the heavy list, and found himself in water up to his waist. From there he was able to reach the store-room and groped about until he found the rack of arms and extracted the shotgun. He was just climbing back into the main cabin when, without warning, the barque's bow slipped off the ledge which had held it and with a terrible crash, fell twelve feet onto the rocks below. Being afloat again, she immediately became upright and for a moment John, caught in the poop, thought it was the end for him. He scrambled out on the deck and heard his father, who had just reached the poop, exclaim: "Thank God" as his ship came free. He knew nothing about his son's escapade and John did nothing to enlighten him. The carpenter got to work with his sounding rod and found ten feet of water in the hold, which meant the barque was in danger of foundering, for the depth of hold was only thirteen feet. The pumps were immediately manned but there was no chanteying this time, for all hands were played out. They worked it with one watch at the pumps, the others getting some sleep, and managed to lower the water level slightly.

At daylight an Eskimo boat was sighted working its way through the ice towards the ship, and soon those on the ship heard the cry "chimo" (welcome) from her crew. When they got alongside, they all kept shouting "thank you ship come". There were six adults, three men and their wives, together with their children and a number of dogs, and the adults were known to the captain of the *Perseverance* through having

worked for him in previous years. Two of them were called
Aa-pa-shu and Too-too, and the latter's wife, Shu-lee, was in
child. After the newcomers had been given coffee, bread
(biscuit), meat, clay pipes and tobacco they relieved the crew of
the pumping and managed to gain a little on the leak. Soon
afterwards the ice holding the ship began to break up, making
it an urgent matter to get the stores landed on the ice back
aboard. Once this had been done, sail was set and the barque
worked her way to a nearby inlet called Nuboyan where it was
hoped a place could be found for beaching the *Perseverance*.
The pumps were kept going the whole time but could do little to
reduce the level of water in the hold. It was obvious there was
a major leak somewhere.

   At Nuboyan, the Eskimo dogs and Too-too's wife Shu-lee
were landed, and a very small tupik (tent), just large enough to
hold the woman, was erected. She crawled into it and was
then left by herself with only the hungry dogs for company, it
being an Eskimo custom to leave a woman alone at such a
time. Boats were sent off to find a suitable place for beaching
the barque so that the forefoot could be repaired, but were
unsuccessful, so the captain decided to sail to the Kikerten
Islands and beach her there. At dawn the next morning, before
leaving for Kekerten, the captain and others went ashore to
bring Shu-loo and her baby aboard. They found her sitting
outside the tupik sewing unconcernedly and when they asked
her where the baby was, were told that after the birth she felt
sick and the dogs broke into the tupik and ate the baby, a
female. She showed them the baby's head, all that the dogs
had left. There was a good deal of doubt about this story, as
infanticide was not uncommon among the Eskimos at that
time, particularly in the case of female children.

   From Nuboyan, the barque set off for Kekerten but was
becalmed about ten miles off her destination. Again the
Eskimos came to their aid, for the vessel had been seen from
the settlement and four whaleboats came off to them. As John
Murray recorded: "Their shouts of welcome were good to hear.
Soon they were all on deck enjoying their coffee and a smoke,
after which we gave them a tow-line from the boom-end and
commenced a long hard pull of six hours before we reached an

anchorage". The barque was beached at Kikerten and it was then found that the forefoot had been smashed into a pulp. The carpenter patched up the damage as best he could with the materials available but when the vessel was refloated she was found to be still leaking badly, half an hour at the pumps every two hours being necessary to keep the water down. This was no great calamity as there were plenty of Eskimos willing to give a hand at the pumps.

It was only now that the full results of the vessels stranding showed up. It was found that sea water had got into all the "bread" (biscuit) tanks on the starboard side, reducing the contents to a mush which had to be shovelled out. It was uneatable for the crew and all was given to the Eskimos, who lined up with sacks, old shirts tied at the sleeves, old skirts and appeared to enjoy the mixture of biscuit and salt water. Other stores, too, were ruined, among them concertinas and melodeons brought for trading purposes whose bellows had been ruined by the water. More serious, much ammunition had been destroyed and altogether the prospects for a winter in the Arctic were not good. Old Tom did not fail to remind the others of the pig's foot and there were certainly grounds for his croaking, for until now the voyage had been one of nothing but ill-luck. And yet, in spite of all they had gone through, the crew were by no means cast down about the prospects of success. Whether the owner, Mr. Kidd of Peterhead, would have shared their optimism seems doubtful, but he was thousands of miles away, unaware of all their misfortunes and would remain so until the ship returned. It was one of the blessings of those pre-wireless days.

The stay at Kekerton while the barque was repaired, was a pleasant one, for the Eskimos were a friendly crowd and many an evening was spent at the Hudson's Bay Company's trading post dancing, at which the Eskimos were quite tireless, to the music of a fiddle or bagpipes. One sad incident marred the stay, an old sick woman, living in a tupik by herself, being worried to death by Eskimo dogs. Her body was, with difficulty, rescued by the Eskimos before the dogs tore it to pieces. Of Eskimo dogs, Captain Murray told me that he always found that by treating them well and feeding them properly they would be good workers. Unfortunately, the Eskimos often treated them badly. In summertime, for example, they would be put on an island where kelp was the only thing to subsist on, with the result that they became ferocious with hunger.

From Kekerten the *Perseverance* sailed across Cumberland Sound to Niantilik Harbour where she found a good anchorage in twenty fathoms of water and immediately set about the business of finding whales. Every morning, weather permitting, all boats left the ship and made fast to suitable places along the ice, a lookout being kept from the highest point. This was called "floe edge whaling" and was a hard, cold job. The men took their food with them, consisting of hard bread (biscuit) and salt meat, working conditions which seem incredibly hard today. But hard though they were, bad luck was with the *Perseverance* all that summer. Several right whales were seen but not one was killed. It looked as though Old Tom's gloomy prophecies were coming more than ever true.

John Murray had another narrow escape that summer. He was away in a kayak late one afternoon, far from the ship, when a big ice-berg suddenly split in two, creating big waves which nearly swamped the tiny kayak. Being out of sight of the ship, he would not have been missed until after dark and would have stood little chance of survival if the kayak had been swamped. Thinking to play a trick on his shipmates, he paddled within sight of the ship and then hid himself inside the kayak. Those aboard, seeing the apparently empty canoe, soon pulled it over only to find young Murray quite safe. There was a good deal of profanity from those in the boat at the trick which had been played on them, and when they got back aboard, the captain had also something to say, much to the point. As his son told me: "The captain gave me a proper doing up and I deserved it".

Eventually, with the young ice forming, and winter not far away, the barque was moved down to Harrison Point, near Blacklead Island, but was still followed by bad luck. While at anchor a small berg got across her bows, causing her to drag, upended her jibboom and smashed all her head gear. About this time, the American whaling schooner *Lizzie P. Simmons* was driven up Cumberland Gulf in an easterly gale and wrecked there, under conditions exactly similar to those in which the *Perseverance* had so narrowly escaped destruction. The crew of the schooner took up their abode at the whaling station on Blacklead Island while the master, Captain Roche, lived in a snow igloo. Captain Roche was a French-Canadian and had shipped some Scottish whalers among his crew, a man called Maitland being one of them. Relations between Captain Roche and some of his crew were not too good, and on one occasion, one of the Scots took his gun from him and used it on the seat of his pants. In actual fact, this was not a very courageous thing to do, since Captain Roche had only one arm, the other having been lost many years before, when a whale line fouled it and tore it off.

With winter coming on, the *Perseverance* was made as safe and comfortable as possible. The masts, yards and even sails were left aloft, snow and ice banked up all round the ship, with ice steps cut in for getting aboard, and as John Murray said: "she was just like the town hall". Every Saturday night, a dance was held in the tweendecks, with Maitland from the *Lizzie P. Simmons* playing the bagpipes and an Eskimo playing on the accordion. As Captain John Murray told me: "At the New Year we had a great time, with the bagpipes going the whole time and the Eskimos dancing till they dropped. As long as the music was going, they danced and never seemed to tire. About half the Eskimo men and woman could play the concertina, so the pipers had a relief at times. One of our Eskimo boat-steerers, Nechaping Jim, could play the fiddle and knew a number of Scottish tunes, and used to direct the dancers in the quadrille, shouting "right" and "left" and "swing your partners" in quite a professional manner".

During the winter, the crew was variously employed in the forenoons, repairing whaling gear, sails or any other job requiring attention, but the short afternoons were free, given over to sledging or playing games. Exercise was an important factor in the winter months if the men were to be kept healthy, and there was very little sickness among the Europeans, but a certain amount among the Eskimos. It was usual to carry a doctor on the Scottish whalers, but this voyage being a wintering one, no doctor was carried, and John's father, the captain, had to be his own medico. Among the Eskimos was a little hunchback called Ashair whom the captain rigged out in the old-time doctor's dress of frock coat and top hat and used him as a messenger to take medicine round to the various sick Eskimos. Ashair made a comical figure as he went off over the ice, but was very proud of himself. The wife of one of the Eskimo harpooners died during the winter and the ship's carpenter had to make a coffin for her. Wood being scarce by this time, he made it rather small, with the result that when they came to put the corpse into it, the only way they could get the lid down, was to stand on it until the carpenter could get the nails in. A somewhat gruesome story, but illustrative of the Eskimos' indifferent attitude towards death.

Even though locked fast in the ice, the *Perseverance*'s winter in the Arctic was by no means free from danger; for although the entire sea surrounding her was frozen over, a large berg grounded alongside the ship, rose and fell with the tide, and at every high water, deposited large quantities of ice on the deck which had to be cleared away immediately. The forefoot, below the ice, still leaked and with the pumps frozen and unworkable, the water had to be baled out of the forepeak with buckets every day right through the winter.

When Spring at last came round again, the boats were prepared for the "floe edge whaling" for another season. They were all hauled out on the ice, painted and overhauled, and in April were taken on sledges about twenty miles down Cumberland Sound to the point where there was ice-free water. But once again the ship's bad luck persisted and not a single whale was caught, although they got fast to one and lost it. The harpooner fired at it with his harpoon gun and missed, and then got a hand harpoon into it which drew after the whale had taken out to a full length of line. Old Tom was in the boat and did not fail to bring up the subject of the pig's foot. He had long ago given up any hope of success on the voyage.

It was well on in the season before the barque at last got a fish. They had by this time left the floe edge and one of the Eskimo harpooners got fast to a large whale which immediately plunged and took out three lines. When it surfaced again, they got a second harpoon into it which made it blow blood and the second mate's boat, in which John Murray was, then approached to finish it off by lancing. There was a light wind blowing at the time and the boat being to leeward of the whale, the men were soon covered in gore and the boat nearly swamped with it. But this was a matter of small importance for they had at last secured a whale. As things turned out, it was the only one they caught and saved them from the ignominy of arriving back in Peterhead a "clean" ship—one which had not caught a single whale. It was some consolation that this whale gave nearly twenty-eight tons of oil and thirty-three hundredweight of whalebone, which was the heaviest head of bone ever landed in Scotland by any whaler.

CHAPTER THREE

TO CALIFORNI-O

JOHN Murray left the *Perseverance* after this voyage, but was to see plenty of her later. It would seem that he had had enough of whaling for a bit, for he next joined a very different kind of ship. This was the steel barque *Helenslea*, built in 1882 by Alexander Stephens & Co. of Dundee for themselves. Messrs. Stephens couldn't have been superstitious, for the *Helenslea* in which John Murray sailed, was the second ship of that name owned by them, the earlier one being an iron barque they built in 1879 which had been lost in 1881. She sank after a collision with the Cunard steamer *Catalonia* near Queenstown at the end of her maiden voyage. Stephens' *Helenslea* was named after the home of Alexander Stephens at West Ferry, near Dundee. There was also another ship with an almost identical name, the wooden full rigged ship *Helenslee*, built at Dumbarton in 1862 for Patrick Henderson and latterly owned in New Zealand.

John joined the *Helenslea* in Liverpool in December 1886, signing on as an AB but living in the half deck and being treated as an apprentice. The decks were covered with snow when he joined the ship and although he was no stranger to far colder conditions than Liverpool could produce at its chilliest, he recorded that he felt colder in the half deck of the *Helenslea* than he had ever done in the Arctic. The master of the barque was Captain James Reid from John Murray's own home town of Peterhead who had taken the vessel from the stocks and made a fine maiden passage of 76 days, Middlesborough to Melbourne, during which time the royals were never taken in. The mate was a Mr. K. who had earlier been in Nova Scotian ships and was later mate of the four-masted barque

Galena, also owned by Stephens. The second mate was a Mr. Blackburn, and the senior apprentice acting third mate was called Hunter. He was later marine superintendent for a Canadian company. There were four apprentices: Adams (later a whaling master), Anderson, King and Shearer. Shearer later lost his life in the barque *Taymount*, lost with all hands on her maiden voyage.

In Liverpool the *Helenslea* loaded a general cargo for San Francisco which included railway iron, block tin and coke. While towing down the Mersey, a dense fog came down and they had to anchor, a lookout being posted to ring the bell every two minutes as per regulations. One of the apprentices was on lookout and kept watch standing on the forehatch. He rang the bell, hanging at the break of the focslehead, by bending a line onto the lanyard so that he could ring it while keeping his hands in his pockets. He was keeping his watch in this manner when he became aware of a knocking on the hatch he was standing on. He reported this to the mate on watch, and on the hatch being opened, two stowaways emerged. They proved to be a boilermaker and a rivetter who for some reason, were very anxious to get to San Francisco. The next day, the fog having lifted, the tug resumed towing them and cast off the towline at Holyhead. At that time, a heavy sea was running and the tug could not get alongside to take off the two stowaways, so as it transpired, they achieved their objective and reached San Francisco. But there must have been a few times during the passage, when they regretted having stowed away, for as will be seen, the *Helenslea* was not an easy ship to sail in.

There were about twelve AB's in the crew, including the following: two Englishmen, Bob and George; two Scots; one Welshman, Hugh Pugh; one Liverpool Irishman; one Dutchman, known for some reason as Pedro; one Russian-Finn, Vidor; one Norwegian; one Greek, "George"— Greeks always seem to be called George. Thus, there was at least half the foremast crowd British, which was a good proportion for a crew picked up in Liverpool in the late '80's. The steward was a negro. The Liverpool Irishman soon showed himself up as the focsle bully and the would-be "cock of the focsle", boasting of the boarding house masters he had slugged. The "cock of the focsle" was a familiar figure in sailing ship days, when on long passages, one man, either by his personality or his pugilistic ability, came to be recognised as the men's leader. But the "cock of the focsle" and the focsle bully are not necessarily the same thing, as was shown in the *Helenslea*. It was not long after sailing, when the Liverpool Irishman called John Murray the particularly foul name—"a son of a whore". John called him out—and he wouldn't fight! After that, his dominance was largely gone, but later, the stowaway boilermaker also challenged him, and again he would not fight. After that, no-one took any notice of his blustering, and on arrival in San Francisco, he was one of the first to desert.

In the North Atlantic, the *Helenslea* sighted a famous little ship, the tea clipper *Titania*, which after being driven out of the tea trade by steamers, was bought by the Hudson's Bay Company and put in the hard trade round the Horn to Vancouver. In spite of her small size, she was in this trade for ten years, before being sold in the early nineties to an Italian firm. Another vessel, spoken on this passage, was the well known American Down Easter, *Edward O'Brien*, built at Thomaston, Maine, in 1882 and stated by Lubbock as being the biggest sailing ship constructed there. She was a ship of 2271 gross tons, named after her builder, Edward E. O'Brien and was known as the "big Edward" to distinguish her from another of the same name, built at Thomaston by O'Brien in 1863, and known as the "little Edward". Lloyd's Register for 1889/90, gives the two vessels, both of them wooden full-rigged ships, built at Thomaston by O'Brien which one would think must have led to some confusion at times. The "big Edward" is entered as owned by Edward O'Brien, the "little Edward" by David Oliver, and it was a Captain D. Oliver who was in command of the "big Edward" when she got her name in the Red Record on at least two occasions. The Red Record was a list of 63 cases of brutal treatment given to seamen aboard American sailing ships in the late 1880's and 1890's and was compiled by a young Scots American called Walter Macarthur, when he was editor of the San Francisco "Coast Seamans' Journal".

Getting down to the Horn in the early part of 1887, (Autumn down there), the *Helenslea* had a bad time of it, being no less than three weeks getting round into the Pacific. Through the short grey days and long black nights of screaming wind and driving snow, there was comfort for no-one, and again Captain Murray has recorded that if he could have got out of her then he would have left the sea for good. But hardships were soon forgotten when they had got round the corner and were in fine weather again, and the rest of the voyage to San Francisco was made without any outstanding incidents.

The anchor had not been down for long in Frisco Harbour before the inevitable boarding-house masters and their runners were aboard. They followed the crew into the focsle and plied them with drink, and within a short time two-thirds of the crew, some of them already half-drunk, staggered out with their bags and accompanied the crimps ashore. A boarding-house master called Murray, got most of the men. By the time the *Helenslea* had berthed in Folsom Street Wharf, there were only four men left in the focsle: the Welshman Pugh, a Scot called Andrew Moir, an Irishman and the Russian-Finn Vidor. The Scot, Moir, a Dundee or Peterhead man, was somewhat out of his element aboard the *Helenslea*, being really a whaler and therefore having a good deal in common with John Murray. He had been aboard the whaler *Cornwallis* when she was lost in the Arctic, her crew being distributed among various other vessels nearby. Moir had been put aboard a Newfoundland sealer and later landed at St. John's NFL. From there he got across to Liverpool, intending to return to his home in Scotland, but got adrift and ended up aboard the *Helenslea*.

Every day while lying alongside, the crimps would go aboard and try to persuade the rest of the crew to leave, but Moir in particular, would not listen to him. On the contrary, he told them they were nothing but a crowd of bloodsuckers, making a fat living out of poor sailormen. The crimps just laughed and told him: "all right, Scottie, we'll get a hold of you yet". "No damn fear you won't", replied Moir, "I'll see to that". But he was wrong. The time came when the *Helenslea*'s cargo was discharged and she was towed away from the wharf to an anchorage at Sausalito, close inside the Golden Gate. Just before she unberthed, Moir ran up to the saloon at the end of the wharf to have a schooner of beer and got back to find the ship moving away from the wharf and already too far away for him to jump it, so was left standing. And that was how the crimp's prophesy came true, for Moir never did get back aboard. The following day, he came off in a boarding house master's boat, the runner rowing and Moir steering. He was not allowed aboard, but his gear was handed down to him and that was the last the *Helenslea* saw of him. Years later, John went aboard a whaler at Dundee and found Moir baling out one of her tanks. He told John, that he was not ashore in San Francisco for long before he was shanghaied aboard an American three-skysail-yarder where, before she reached New York, he saw plenty of "belaying pin soup" being handed out.

The *Helenslea* lay in Sausalito Bay for about two months and it was during this time, that John Murray first met John Pearson of Tayport, Fife, who was then second mate of another of Stephens' ships, the four-masted barque *Earl of Dalhousie.**

The master of this ship was the well-known Captain John Jarvis, of Tayport, who later invented a brace-winch, which greatly eased the work of bracing the yards of big sailing ships, a fitting which was taken up more by German ships than by British. Captain Jarvis had the *Earl of Dalhousie* on her previous voyage, her maiden one, during which she had capsized in 'Frisco harbour, fortunately without loss of life. He had raised and re-rigged the ship himself and she was none the worse for the mishap. The *Helenslea* was lying at Sausalito at the time of Queen Victoria's Golden Jubilee on June 20th, 1887 and was the only British ship in port which did not give her crew a holiday. Even the American ships recognised the occasion and gave their men the day off. The apprentices of the *Helenslea*, together with young Murray, were sent off to get water from a well and on the way dropped the mate at a saloon called the "Cottage by the Sea", built out on a wharf with the water directly beneath it, just the place incidentally, which was favoured by the crimps, who could drop their drunken or doped victims through the floor into a boat waiting below.

Having filled up their water casks, the lads of the *Helenslea* went back to the "Cottage by the Sea" to pick up the mate, who, when he finally appeared was somewhat drunk. On the

*See page 000 for further mention of John Pearson

way back to the ship, he was standing up in the boat to cheer the big ferry steamer *San Rafael* when he overbalanced and toppled into the water and had to be fished out. In Sausalito, there was a saloon kept by a former professional heavyweight boxer called Paddy Ryan, which was the mate's favourite haunt. The period laid up at Sausalito was a pleasant one for the apprentices and what remained of the crew, for they could get ashore most evenings. The cook had deserted along with the focsle hands and King, one of the apprentices, acted in his place during the lay-up. Up on Kearney Street was a saloon called the "White Wings", kept by a Britisher named Tregella, presumably a Cornishman, who had at one time been at sea in British ships. A schooner of beer at Tregella's place cost five cents, with which one got a free lunch, and the appetites of the lads from the hungry *Helenslea* soon produced from the proprietor the remark that he was glad there weren't many like them for eating. Electricity was then something of a novelty and the bar rail of the "White Wings" was wired, so that the barman, by pressing a button, could send a current along it and give the patrons a shock. One of the prominent boarding house masters in San Francisco at that time was Murray. His namesake aboard the *Helenslea* often saw him or his runners and was actually offered a job in charge of one of Murray's boats. He was told that the only thing he had to do was keep sober, otherwise he would be shanghaied, as he undoubtedly would have been.

After laying up for about two months, the *Helenslea* was chartered to run coal from Departure Bay, Vancouver Island, to San Diego, California, and it was now that Captain Reid and his officers started having trouble—crew trouble. The men who had deserted had to be replaced, and the only way that could be done was through the boarding house masters—the crimps. This was routine in San Francisco and the other American ports in the Pacific North-west. But, where in the majority of ships, the articles were foreign, in the case of the *Helenslea* she was now regarded as a coaster and the new men had to be signed on coasting articles, which called for American rates of pay, a much better scale of food than in British ships, and quite different conditions of work. The differences to be expected were apparent when the new crew joined, for where it was usual in almost any port for a crew to join the ship drunk, these men swaggered aboard anything but helpless and even brought their own cook, a Chinaman, with them.

From the moment they stepped aboard there was trouble. The apprentices were just sitting down to their midday meal of pea soup and salt pork, when the new men passed the open door of the halfdeck. Their leader, a long, lean individual called Belasco, or "Bob", stopped at the door and looked with disgust at the food. "Jesus Christ, do you eat those things?", he asked, looking at the pantiles. "Here, let's have a look at one", and taking a biscuit threw it aft along the deck, towards the poop. It was a challenge, if there ever was one. "Here, give me another", and again threw a biscuit along aft. "What d'you keep them in?" he next asked, and on being shown the bread barge, seized it and threw the whole lot along the deck. The mate of any ship is, under the captain, responsible for the maintenance of discipline aboard, and on the outward passage, the mate of the *Helenslea*, who had sailed in Nova Scotian ships, where discipline was very strictly enforced, had shown himself something of a "hard case". As John Murray put it: "one shout from the mate and the crew would be climbing over one another to be first on deck", and it can be taken as quite certain that the mate was no "paper tiger". The apprentices, knowing this, expected the mate to be out on deck in one bound after the incident of the biscuit throwing, but it was some little time before he appeared. When he did, he called out to Belasco: "Here, long fellow, I want to talk to you". Belasco turned and drawled out: "Looka here, mister, my name ain't 'long fellow'. You take a look in that little book of yours and maybe you'll find it".

"I don't give a damn what your name is. Get those pieces of bread off the deck and over the side", the mate said.

The man Belasco appears to have been a character who would have fitted well into an Ernest Hemingway novel, a quiet, slow-speaking, cold-blooded individual. He said: "Mister mate, if you want those pieces of bread thrown over the side, the best bloody thing you can do, is do it yourself". At this point, another of the crew came up and put his hand familiarly on the mate's shoulder, saying: "the best thing you can do, mister, is get the hell aft and stay there—our crowd is all one". There were seven Americans among the crew, with one cockney, a rather poor type who, having been in the States a few months, talked with an exaggerated American accent and thought himself a real hard case. This man now joined the group and started swearing at the mate in his cockney-American. This was probably the point at which the after-guard had their last opportunity of asserting their authority. It was not taken and from then on the American members of the crew had things very much their own way. They retired to the focsle and started a drinking bout and were left to themselves. Later the mate went to the focsle door and told the men to turn to at trimming the ballast in preparation for sailing but was told to "take yer damn nose out of that door or you'll get a boot thrown at it. We'll trim no ballast today". The English dictionary defines mutiny as "open revolt against constituted authority" and the sorry events related here must surely come under this definition. One cannot help wondering why they were tolerated, but tolerated they were.

One is reminded of a somewhat similar situation which is recounted by J. Inches Thomson in his book "Voyages and Wanderings in Far Off Seas and Lands". In Sydney, Australia, the author chartered an American barque called the *Ruby* and accompanied the vessel to San Francisco. On arrival, the vessel was of course boarded by the crimps, of whom Thomson remarks that "the audacity and daring of the San Francisco crimps at that period, showed itself in defiance of all law. One of the gang, well dressed and with faultless linen, was hanging about the cabin door. Captain Van Norden asked him what he wanted, and was informed with a 'guess' and a drawl that he wanted his sailors. 'I don't keep my sailors in the cabin, go for'd out of this', he was told, to which he replied: 'I take no orders from you' and putting his hand in his breast pocket said 'and I never draws but I fires'. The captain did not consider it prudent to continue the argument". That incident had taken place in the 1870's, a little earlier than John Murray's visit in the *Helenslea*, but the same atmosphere of lawlessness and readiness to settle any trouble by violence and the bullet still prevailed.

Early next morning, when orders were given to make fast the tug and man the windlass, the crew refused to turn to until the cook had made them some hot cakes to go with their coffee. Towing out towards the Golden Gate, when the mates were shouting their orders for setting sail, they were asked "what the hell they were making all the noise about". At breakfast time, the men came along in a body, headed by Belasco. They stood round the cabin door and shouted: "Come out old man, we want to talk to you". Captain Reid appearing, they told him it was Thursday morning and they wanted their ham and eggs.

"But I have no ham and eggs aboard here for you" the captain said. "Cap., you know the rules on the coast, that the crew is entitled to ham and eggs Thursday and Sunday" and here they were within their rights. Captain Reid compromised and gave them the best he could with the stores aboard, and for the moment, peace was restored. But not for long. The coloured steward went along to the galley that forenoon and seeing the Chinese cook peeling the potatoes for dinner, asked who he was peeling them for. "For the men" replied the cook.

"no, no, you don't peel potatoes for sailors".

"Me savvy, me savvy" the Chinaman replied impatiently.

"You no savvy", replied the negro, and eventually persuaded the cook that there was no need for all that work of peeling potatoes for sailors. The apprentices were in the halfdeck at dinner time when they heard screams coming from the galley nearby and went out to see the cook with the kit of potatoes upside down on his head and one of the sailors hanging on to his pigtail and kicking him around the galley. Not unnaturally, the cook blamed the steward for what had happened and was later heard banging his pots and pans and telling the world he would "cut the throat of that black son of a bitch".

It soon came out that the men signed-on in San Francisco, did not regard themselves as sailors. They said that they were coal shovellers and absolutely refused to do any work other than handling sails, steering, keeping a lookout and washing down the decks of a morning. Such jobs as 'sujeeing' and painting, they said were not part of their job and as such, occupies a good part of a sailor's life at sea, the situation aboard the *Helenslea* at that time must have been extremely unpleasant for the afterguard.

Departure Bay, where the *Helenslea* went to load her coal, lies on the east coast of Vancouver Island, near Nanaimo, of which it is practically a part, and opposite Vancouver. It is by no means an easy place for a sailing ship to make, for the region is one of strong currents and much fog, but in the days when John Murray was there, Departure Bay gave employment to a large number of sailing ships. The great days of the wooden clippers were already past, and many old ships, famous in their day, found employment in the coal trade. The *Glory of the Seas*, one of Donald McKay's most beautiful creations, had entered the trade only a couple of years before John was there, and although he did not mention it, he might well have seen her in 'Frisco or Departure Bay. Among other famous old ships in the coal trade, were the *Dashing Wave*, *Charmer*, *Harry Morse*, *India*, *Jabez Howes* and *Sterling*.

The *Helenslea* arrived at Departure Bay apparently without incident, and was there some time before she got a berth. Nanaimo, to give the place its more general name, had been founded less than forty years before the *Helenslea* went there. In 1851 it was no more than a small Indian village known as Winthuysen Inlet and it was the discovery of coal there in that year, which soon changed it into a busy town. The Hudson's Bay Company had a trading post at Victoria, further south, and once it had been established that coal of good quality and in paying quantities existed at "Winthuysen Inlet, commonly known as Nanymo", the whole area was taken over by the Company. The first shipment of coal left Nanaimo on September 10th, 1852 in the schooner *Cadboro*.

The first miners were mostly Nanaimo Indians, a peaceable people, very different to the warlike Haidas from the northern part of the island, and some Scotsmen who had come out to Vancouver Island in the barque *Harpooner* in 1849 and the barque *Tory* in 1851. Then on November 27th, 1854 there arrived the barque *Princess Royal* of London, with a party of miners from Brierley Hill, Staffordshire. There were twenty-four families, seventy-five people in all. The settlement was known as Colvilletown until 1860, the name being officially altered to Nanaimo in that year. Once the mines had proved workable, more labour was needed and Chinese were brought in. To give some idea of the size of the industry, there were 204 white men, 61 Chinese and 19 Indians working in the mines in 1874, but these figures were soon greatly increased as the mines were developed.

All through the history of the coal mines at Nanaimo, there is constant mention of accidents, and in the year the *Helenslea* was there, a major disaster killed 150 men, followed by another a few months later, which killed 77. There was much trouble of another sort too, for strikes were frequent, sometimes accompanied by violence. Relatively small though Nanaimo was, it gives us a picture of the struggle between Labour and Capitalism which is still a major issue in the world today. But we have progressed since then, apparently, for in 1887 the militia was called in to evict the miners from their homes when they refused to return to work because their claim for higher pay was refused.

Of Departure Bay itself, Captain Murray told me that the population consisted mostly of Indians and Chinese, with a few whites supervising, and there was only one saloon. An old Scotsman, who could usually be found at the saloon, took on a contract to supply a wooden steamer from Alaska with bunker coal, and no other labour being available, asked Captain Reid if he could allow his apprentices to do the work. Permission being granted, the lads were able to earn a little very welcome money, at the rate of fifty cents an hour. There was little in the way of recreation, and the lads of the *Helenslea* sometimes went for a walk in the forest which surrounded the harbour. One evening, they met a man, who it turned out, was an old Navy hand, probably a deserter, as many naval ratings deserted in the area at that time. After solemnly warning them about never giving whisky to the Indians, he invited the crowd from the *Helenslea* along to his home, which turned out to be a small shack on the edge of the forest. On entering, they found the floor of the one room, littered with empty bottles, and an Indian squaw lying on the bed. He was a hospitable old man, and wanting to give them a drink, started searching among the bottles on the floor, for one with something in it. Not finding it, he accused the woman of having stolen his whisky and in spite of her howls, pulled her out of bed to search for a drink. Later they had a sing-song, the old tar starting them off with "pretty Polly Perkins of Paddington Green".

Her coal cargo loaded, the *Helenslea* left Departure Bay for National City, now a part of San Diego, lower California, almost on the frontier with Mexico. The passage appears to have been an uneventful one, but it was not long after arrival before the trouble with the crew, which had never been far below the surface, boiled over. An argument started among the crew as to whether they had to go aft for their sugar ration or whether the steward should bring it to the galley. It was one of those senseless debates, only started by men who are looking for trouble on any pretext. The cockney marched aft with the tin for the sugar, and when the negro steward came to the door, held out the tin with his left hand and then suddenly struck the negro with his right. That started things, for the steward ran into the saloon, grabbed a bayonet from a rack of old arms there, and went for the Cockney, who, true to type, turned and fled. He headed for the focsle, shouting as he went for a gun to "shoot the black son of a bitch" and the steward, knowing what awaited him if he entered the focsle, went no further than the galley. But it was not long before several of the men set about the steward in the galley and gave him a bad beating. Young Murray, standing in the halfdeck door, saw one of them deliberately kicking him in the face with his heavy boots.

As soon as he could, the steward went ashore and complained to the police. Rather surprisingly, one might think, they listened to him and two marshals came back aboard to investigate, and called for one of the men involved to come up out of the hold where they were working. But they would not have one coming up by himself and all hands came up. The two marshals were standing with a sailor between them, listening to the steward's complaints, when suddenly he broke free and butted the poor old steward on the forehead and he went backwards, his feet in the air, showing his lovely red socks. He made a comic sight. Then another of the men made a rush at the second mate, but the marshals grabbed him first.

They did things in a rough and ready manner in those days on the Pacific Coast, and as soon as a judge could be found, a court was convened and the case tried immediately. The steward stated his case, pointing to the large lump on his forehead, but one of the sailors stood up and said: "Don't believe him, Mr. Judge, nothing less than a brick could make a lump like that on a nigger's head". Nevertheless, two of the men were fined, so the rest of the crew clubbed together and paid the fines and everyone left the courtroom.

Later the Americans demanded to be paid off, and although they had signed on for two voyages, the captain was glad to let them go. There seems to have been no doubt that they were a dangerous crowd, to whom authority meant nothing. At any sign of trouble they all banded together, never allowing one of their number to be caught by himself, and, according to John Murray, all had firearms. The only one he was sorry to see depart, was the Chinese cook. "I'd gone ashore with him several nights" he recorded "and had visited an opium den with him and had been introduced to some of his friends. Several times I was invited to have a pipe of opium but always refused".

From National City the *Helenslea* was ordered to Port Townsend, Puget Sound, for orders, and a new crew was signed on. This time Captain Reid signed them on British articles, although with the usual carelessness of seamen, none of the men paid any attention to the clauses gabbled out to them in the consul's office and did not realise what Agreement they were putting their mark to.

It was not long after sailing before Captain Reid discovered that his new crew were no better than the last one. The leader was an Irish-American called O'Brien, a long, lean individual of much the same type as Belasco, who ruled as the undisputed cock of the focsle. Once again, the crew refused to do anything but essential work but this time Captain Reid was in a stronger position and on arrival at Port Townsend, brought a case for refusal of duty against them. Two of the men, O'Brien being one of them, were each fined five dollars and the other man accepted the sentence, but not so O'Brien. He became very abusive, calling the judge a "whisky-nosed parson-faced son of a bitch", to which the judge, no doubt familiar with trouble-some sailors, responded with: "I fine you a further five dollars". But this did not stop the Irishman, who next turned

his attention to Captain Reid. "You long, lean son of a bitch, I'm
going to blow holes in you the first chance I get" he told him.
This resulted in a further five dollars fine and more abuse of
the judge. But even the Irishman had to admit defeat
eventually, and his fines having been paid by the rest of the
crew, they left the courtroom. Soon afterwards all these men
were paid off.

If the Liverpool Irishman shipped at the beginning of the
voyage, had been quickly shown to be a blowhard, there was
nothing of the empty boaster about O'Brien. He was a genuine
specimen of the "hard case", one of the type who until a few
years earlier had manned the hard-driving western ocean
packets and been known and feared by many, as the "packet
rats". They were the men described by Captain Samuel
Samuels, famous packet ship commander, as "the toughest
class of men in all respects. They could stand the worst
weather, food and usage and put up with less sleep, more rum
and harder knocks, than any other sailors . . . they had not the
slightest idea of morality, or honesty, and gratitude was not in
them. The dread of the belaying pin was the only thing that
kept them in subjection. I tried to humanize these brutal
natures as much as possible, but the better they were treated
the more trouble my officers had with them". Shortly before
joining the *Helenslea*, O'Brien had been a boarding house
runner in Port Townsend. It was said that he had gone aboard a
sailing ship there and taken the whole crew out of her at the
point of a revolver and his threat to "blow holes" in Captain
Reid was not just an empty one. Before leaving the *Helenslea*
he told the captain he'd "have every damn man out of you
before you leave". The only good figure among the crew picked
up at National City was the cook, whom John described as the
best one he had ever seen aboard a ship. "Flash Jack" was his
sobriquet and he could make a meal out of anything. After his
departure with the rest in Port Townsend, the *Helenslea* was
left with three men in her focsle and no cook, one of the
apprentices taking on this thankless job again.

From Port Townsend, the barque was towed to Port Gamble
by the tug *Tyhee* to load lumber for Melbourne. Port Gamble is
one of the many small ports on Puget Sound which sprang into

being because they were in the centre of one of the largest pine forests in the world and were well situated for the shipping of wood. Today it has a population of less than a thousand, but when John Murray was there, it consisted of a sawmill and a few wooden shacks, with the inhabitants a mixture of Indians, Chinese and white loggers.

Christmas Eve 1887, found the *Helenslea* lying alongside an American wooden ship. It was freezing hard and with nothing at all to take them ashore, the half deck crowd of the barque gathered round the focsle bogie stove for a singsong. They were sitting there when the door burst open and a very drunken youth fell inside. He was the cabin boy of the American ship and had with him a demijohn of whisky which he invited them to share. They were glad to do so, for it was a pretty cheerless Christmas Eve, but the results were unfortunate. Not used to drinking whisky, they treated it rather incautiously, swigging it down from enamel mugs, these being the only drinking receptacles they had, with the result that they all got drunk. A new cook, a cockney, had joined the day before and later told John Murray that he had lain in his bunk scared to death of the "wild Scotsmen". The next day there were few in a fit state to accept the invitation of the proprietor of the settlement's only saloon to a free lunch, but John Murray and one or two others went along. At the saloon, they found things hardly in accordance with the spirit of peace on earth, an Irishman and a Norwegian being engaged in combat when they arrived. It was a brutal affair and before he finally knocked him out, the Irishman had reduced the Norwegian's face to a red pulp. Such affairs were apparently of common occurrence, for others sitting there playing cards, did not even look up, and a couple of men coming in, just rolled the unconscious body to one side with their feet.

There was at that time a heavy penalty for anyone supplying an Indian with liquor, although the latter got round the law easily enough by bribing white men to get it for them. On his way back to the ship, young Murray was accosted by a white man with the following proposition: "There's an Indian over there with a bottle of whisky in his pocket. I'll challenge him to a wrestling match, he'll take off his coat, you get the bottle and i'll meet you down at the wharf later". What would have happened if the Indian had won, the man did not say, but his proposal was not taken up. There can have been little crime in Port Gamble in those days, or the laws were very liberally administered, for there was only one marshal, or policeman, an elderly man who worked in the sawmill by day, and spent his evenings in the saloon .

When the lumber cargo had been loaded, the *Helenslea* towed down to Port Townsend, about twenty miles away, and anchored to await a crew. Almost inevitably, the men were helplessly drunk when they came aboard, and remembering O'Brien's threat to "have every damn man out of you before you sail" Captain Reid got a marshal down on board. That night the marshall handed the watchman a rifle and told him: "Fire at any boat that doesn't answer to your hail the third time". Then as an afterthought added: "You'd better call me before you fire". Those were wild days on the West Coast and the Law of the gun was all-powerful. Of the area, Basil Lubbock wrote: "Seattle in the '90's was a tough little spot where you could lose your money in double quick time at faro, roulette or stud poker; where you could be shot for refusing a drink of fire-water. This was the lure that emptied the focsles of the sailing ships in the late '90's and caused the crimps of Seattle and Tacoma to outdo their celebrated rival of San Francisco and Portland in the matter of "shanghai-ing".

The *Helenslea* had finished off her cargo with a big deck load, something detested by seafarers because it took up all the deck space and hampered movement. Some shipowners, Captain George Duncan of the *Empires* among them, would not carry a deck cargo, saying that a ship so loaded was not seaworthy, and there was a very clear illustration of this aboard the *Helenslea* off Cape Flattery. Caught in a squall under full sail, she went right over on her beam ends and very nearly capsized before the loss of many of the upper sails eased the pressure and brought her upright again. This accident would never have happened had the sheets and halliards been readily available instead of half-buried in a huge stack of wood.

The passage to Melbourne was otherwise uneventful and the crew shipped at Port Townsend was found to be a good one once the liquor was out of them. But there was more trouble as soon as they anchored off Sandridge Pier. The morning after arrival, the bell was struck for the men to turn-to and when no-one appeared, the third mate went for'd to investigate. The men then accused him of having "flogged the clock", meaning he had advanced it to get more work out of them. This being reported to the mate, he also went for'd and into the focsle, where one of the men threatened him with a marline spike. A fight followed, in the course of which the sailor, with the mate on top of him, bit his nose so badly as to nearly sever it from his face. A boat was put in the water and the mate was taken to hospital to have his nose sewn up. As John Murray said: "the mate's nose was no beauty before and now it looked almost like a half moon". The seaman was arrested, tried and given the option of a heavy fine or three months in prison, so he chose the latter. He did this as a way of getting out of the ship, for he knew that if he stayed in her, he could expect nothing but trouble with the mate whose nose he had bitten. Having been signed-off, he paid his fine and was free.

There seems to be no doubt that at this time, the *Helenslea* was a hard ship to sail in. There were few holidays for the halfdeck and on a Saturday it was generally late before they finished cleaning brasswork and scrubbing decks. As John Murray said: "It was rather aggravating when we could see the apprentices from the above vessels bound for an enjoyable afternoon ashore". Towards the end of their stay in Melbourne, John Murray decided that he'd had enough of the ship and made preparations to desert. The day before they were due to sail for Newcastle, he had his gear packed ready and put in his bunk with the curtains drawn so that the others would not know of his intentions, intending to clear out that night. Unfortunately for his plans, the time of sailing was advanced unexpectedly and he lost his opportunity. Such unimportant items, as a sailing time advanced a few hours, can alter the whole course of a man's life and may well have done so in the case of John Murray. At any rate, he completed the voyage instead of clearing out in Australia.

In Newcastle, the barque loaded coal for Valparaiso and arrived at the Chilean port soon after a reservoir on a mountain top there had burst and caused great damage. The coal cargo was discharged by the crew, whose day finished at 6 p.m., but the apprentices, after working all day, had then to take the captain ship-visiting. If they did not get back until after 10 p.m., the mate allowed them to sleep in till seven bells, 7.20 a.m. but as the captain usually got back just before 10 p.m., they generally had to turn out ready to start work at 6 a.m.

After discharging her coals, the *Helenslea* sailed the 400 miles up to Caldera to load copper ore for Swansea: she became a "copper ore man" for a passage. The loading process was very slow and the mate had difficulty finding work for the crew. They spent a lot of time with chipping hammers in the hold, over the side, and even dragged old chains up from the forepeak, to chip them. And yet, difficult though it was to find work for the crew, the apprentices were not given a holiday when New Year's Day (1889) came round. At least two of the crew, Murray and an apprentice, decided that they would have a holiday, come what may, and volunteered to go ashore for the ship's provisions. Once ashore, they left the third occupant of the boat to sail back to the ship on his own, and set off to see the sights, such as they were. After wandering around for some time, they came across a sailor from their ship, who had a mournful tale to tell. He had had a few drinks ashore the previous night and, getting down to the wharf to find no boat there, had laid down to sleep. He must have slept soundly, for when he woke up, he found that he had been stripped of his good go-ashore suit and left with an old mantilla and sombrero. When he managed to get back aboard the mate sacked him, telling him to get his clothes and leave the ship.

"I don't know how I'll get out of this place" he told the boys. "Very few ships come here. I've met a few hard ones but that mate is about the hardest". The two of them were still talking to the sailor when they saw the mate, who had gone ashore to find them after the boat had returned with only one man in it. Coming up, he ordered them back aboard. "The boat is waiting there, get back aboard and turn to".

"If I go back aboard I'll do no work today", Murray assured him. "It's the New Year and no-one is expected to work today. The work we've been doing is unnecessary, anyway".

"If you don't get back aboard I'll see you in jail", the mate threatened them.

Filled with a sense of injustice, Murray said: "All right, lead on" and the two of them followed the mate along to the prison. The mate knew no Spanish but by pointing at Murray and the apprentice and then to the inside of the jail he soon got the vigilante on the gate, to understand that he wanted them arrested. Things happened quickly then, and very soon the two were inside, with the gate shut and the mate jeering at them through the bars.

"You damn fools" he said, "I hope you will have a happy New Year there!" By this time he had forfeited the right to any respect from them and the apprentice told him to "take that chewed-up nose of yours out of it", a reference to his facial beauty which so enraged the mate that he stood there shaking the bars of the jail until the vigilantes told him he'd better go if he didn't want to be inside with the others.

The two soon found that the jail consisted of a large walled rectangle, really a fort, with cells on two sides of it, the building serving the double purpose of prison and madhouse. There were several lunatics wandering about freely among the prisoners and one poor crazed creature in particular singled out the two from the *Helenslea* following them round with a long nail in one hand and a dagger-like piece of broken glass in the other. He never approached them closer than six feet or so, stopping when the did and staring at the ground until they moved on, when again he would shamble after them. As was usual in those days in South American jails, no food was supplied to the prisoners, and they had to rely on outsiders to bring it to them. A request by the two to see the British Consul produced nothing more than a blank stare, and at the end of the day there were two very hungry youths from the *Helenslea* in Caldera jail. Apart from being within the prison walls they were left to roam about as they pleased and, when darkness fell they looked round for a cell which was comparatively clean and, if possible, free from lice, with which the jail was infested. Having found one, they spent an extremely uncomfortable night and the next morning, being now twenty-four hours without any food, again attempted to contact the British

Consul. This still produced no more than a stare until one of
the warders suddenly exclaimed; "Ah! Eengleesh Consul eh?".
As a result John's companion was allowed to go and see the
Consul and later that day they received some food. Captain
Reid also came to the jail with a clerk from the Consul's office
and had the two released. Thus ended an incident which, most
unpleasant at the time, became softened with the passage of
the years into an escapade of youth.

Copper ore is very heavy and the regular copper ore traders,
which nearly all hailed from Swansea, were fitted with a
special trunk, very strongly built, to raise the weight of the
cargo and thus reduce the excessive "stiffness" which pro-
duces a quick violent roll. The *Helenslea* had no such trunk and
loaded the cargo pyramid fashion, to raise the weight, as is
done with a nitrate cargo. People at Caldera shook their heads
pessimistically and declared she would never reach Swansea
with the cargo so loaded. But they were wrong, and the
Helenslea arrived safely after an average passage. She had
been away nearly two and a half years during which she had
carried five cargoes, which was not a bad average.

John Murray left the *Helenslea* at Swansea and went home
to Peterhead. Captain Reid remained in the barque until he
took over the new four-masted barque *Galena*, built in 1890 at
Dundee by Alexander Stephens & Co., for their own use. He
was still alive in 1930, living at Aberdeen. The *Helenslea* was
sold in 1895 to Chadwick, Wainwright & Co. but only lasted a
year or so under their house-flag, being wrecked on Inaccessi-
ble Island, Tristan da Cunha, in 1897. This long and eventful
voyage of John's in the *Helenslea* was the first and last of its
kind he made, and the only one in which he crossed the
equator.

CHAPTER FOUR

BACK TO THE WHALERS

AFTER a holiday, John joined his first steamship, the *Cairngorm*, a small vessel owned in Leith, as an A.B. Of this ship he had nothing good at all to say. She had no power, the food was atrocious, it was impossible to steer her properly and the course she used to make he described as a "four-pointed star". He had joined her only to put in time until the whaling season came round again and was glad to leave her.

It was back to the whalers again after this, as an A.B. in the steam whaling barque *Esquimaux*, of Dundee. She was a vessel of 593 gross tons built by Alexander Stephens at Dundee in 1865 as a ship and was reduced to a barque rig in 1883. On this question of rig in the whalers, one finds a radical difference of opinion as expressed by two authors of books on whaling. In "The Gateway to the Polynia" by Captain John C. Wells, R.N. (1873) he states flatly that "it is essentially necessary that a vessel frequenting the Arctic seas should be full-rigged, and able to sail in case of a breakdown of the engines or running short of coal, when the vessel would be in a safe condition to prosecute her voyage". But in the book "A Whaling Cruise to Baffin's Bay" by Commander Albert Hastings Markham, R.N. written in 1875, he just as flatly states that "the whalers are generally ship-rigged, which I consider to be a great mistake, a barque being far more handy". He adds a footnote that "as soon as the whalers arrive on their fishing grounds the mizen topsail is invariable unbent and stowed away". It is not out of place to add that neither of the men whose opinions are given above were whalers. It is regrettable that I did not ask Captain Murray for his opinion on this point.

The *Esquimaux*'s best known commander was Captain Charles Yule, who had her from the time she was built until 1879.

In 1883 he became Harbourmaster of Dundee and held this responsible position until 1920, when he was 85, and died in 1935 at the age of 100. The *Esquimaux*, a sister ship to the steam whaling barques *Erik* and *Arctic (I)* was enormously strongly built, with 8½ feet of solid timber in her bows. She burned 7½ tons of coal a day for the good speed of 8½ knots,

"ESQUIMAUX"

and was the largest whaler in which John Murray served. She had been built for the Dundee Seal and Whale Fishing Company, in which Stephens had a controlling interest and there can be no doubt that in the 1860s and 1870s sealing and whaling was a very profitable business. An indication of this is the fact that although shipbuilding remained their main business, A. Stephen & Sons had their own boiling yard (for reducing blubber into oil) in Dundee, and a member of the firm had his own tannery for curing seal skins. In the early 1870s, also, the company started their own yard at St. John's NFL for dealing with seal skins.

"POLYNIA"

The early eighties saw the end of the good days for Scottish whaling and by the time John Murray joined the *Esquimaux* Stephens had sold her to D. Bruce of Dundee who had a large fleet of cargo-carrying sailing vessels and one other whaler, the steam barque *Polynia*. Messrs. Stephens kept two whalers, the *Aurora* and the *Terra Nova*, both of them to become famous in polar exploration.

In the *Esquimaux*, John Murray went across to Newfoundland to take part in the sealing from there, which as a result of the growing scarcity of the Greenland Right whale had become normal procedure with Scottish whalers. The master of the ship at this time was Captain W. F. Milne, who had had her since 1883. Leaving Peterhead in early 1890 the *Esquimaux* battled her way across the North Atlantic to St. John's and there prepared for the sealing. The ship's eight whale boats were put ashore and a number of punts taken aboard in their place. The decks were sheathed with planks of wood, to protect them from the "sparables" (spikes) on the boots of the extra men, known as sweilers, who would be taken aboard for the sealing, and much of the ship's bunker coal was put ashore to make room for the anticipated catch of seals. In the old days there was no limit to the number of sweilers a ship could take, and in 1892 the *Terra Nova*, slightly larger than the *Esquimaux*, took 352, which was considered exceptional. In 1898 legislation was brought in governing the number of extra men a sealer could take. Bunks were put up in the tweendecks for the sweilers, about 300 in number, and the living conditions for such a large crowd in such cramped quarters were rough, to put it mildly.

To a Newfoundlander, seals were "swiles", from whence came the word "sweiler" for sealer. The seals which were the objective of the annual hunt were hair seals of two types, the harp, so called because of the marking on the backs of the adults, and the hood, which has a large inflatable sac on the nose of the male. The harp, much more numerous than the hood, is timorous by nature and will leave its young when attacked, but the hood is a different proposition. The sac on the nose which gives the seal its name can be inflated so hard, that it used to be a tradition that it would turn a bullet, and unlike the harp, the hoods of both sexes will fight to the death in defence of their young, as many a sealer has learned. The young of both species are born at the end of February or beginning of March and the process takes place with such regularity that the Newfoundland Government was able to fix dates before which no sealer was allowed to leave port for the sealing grounds. This was done to give the seals a chance to develop and thus save the species from extermination. Sailing vessels were allowed to leave port on March 1st, vessels with engines had to wait until March 10th.

The official time for leaving St John's on March 10th was eight o'clock in the morning and at that time the harbour must have been a wonderful sight with twenty or more sealers of various rigs and types all making for the narrows, the 860-feet wide entrance to the port. If it was a hard winter, the harbour would still be frozen over and the ships would have to be pulled through the ice by sheer brute force, with hundreds of sweilers all hauling on hawsers leading ahead, while others ran from side to side to roll the ship and help to break the ice. As regards the commander of the ship when sealing, some of the Scottish vessels had a Newfoundlander in charge while others preferred to keep the regular captain. In their own ships which went to the sealing, Alexander Stephen generally retained the regular captain.

The sweilers themselves were a particularly tough and hardy crowd, drawn to the sealing from all over Newfoundland at a time of year when there was little other work for them. According to one writer, the "voyage to the ice" as the sealing was called, was almost a picnic, despite the real dangers and hardships, and men would walk, sail or row from far distant outposts for the chance of a place aboard one or another of the ships. Doctor Lindsay in "A Voyage to the Arctic on the Whaler *Aurora*" in 1884 remarks: "When one saw this small army of fine-looking hard-working and very poor men he could not help being sorry that their forefathers in emigrating had not gone a little further and settled in Canada or the U.S.A., instead of on this inhospitable land . . . . Newfoundland meant to every one of them a life of toil with not much more hope than the mother country could have given them. Poor soil and a relentless winter mean this as a rule in a country the mineral resources of which have not been developed".

The two ships almost being identical in size, conditions aboard the *Aurora* must have been much the same as those aboard the *Esquimaux* and I again quote Dr. Lindsay. On March 11th, the day after leaving St. John's, he tells us: "I looked into the 'tweendecks and saw a horrible mess. The bunks were full of men, many playing cards, as each bunk held four. They must have been stifled. For light, lamps burning seal oil were used, and the reek coming from the main hatch would almost have suggested fire". With most of those sweilers certainly smoking down in those crowded 'tween decks, the dangers of fire must have been very real; and yet, although the rate of loss among the sealing vessels was terribly high, fire does not seem to have been one of the main causes, despite the fact that the timbers of these old ships must have been positively soaked in oil.

To adequately feed hundreds of men aboard vessels as small as the whalers, was obviously impossible and all they were given was sea biscuit and "pinnacle tea" with pork and duff served three times a week. "Pinnacle tea" was tea made with water obtained from pinnacles of fresh water ice, the splinters being put into a tank, tea added and steam turned on, molasses taking the place of milk and sugar. Such a diet was not enough for men who had to work hard in bitter cold, but the sweilers got plenty of nourishment, if of the crudest kind. Once among the seals they had the livers, hearts and flippers of the creatures in an inexhaustible supply, and would carry them hanging on their belt like scalps and eat them cooked, or raw when hungry. Often they would lower a liver into a pot of boiling tea to thaw it out so that they could eat it. This was certainly living life in the raw, about as hard as it could be and very dangerous, for not very high rewards. The "sculp" or skin of a seal was worth at the time of John Murray's first visit to the sealing about two and a half dollars (approximately ten shillings) and the sweilers received one third of the entire catch. Supposing a ship to have killed 20,000 seals, which brought about £10,000, one third of which would go to the sweilers, of whom there might be 250. This gives a figure of only about £13 per man, for perhaps weeks of intensely hard and dangerous work which annually took many lives. And very many sealers killed nothing like this number.

In his book "The Log of Bob Bartlett" Captain Robert A. Bartlett gives us some facts about the rewards the sealers got: "Getting a load usually takes about six weeks. You'd think this would bring a lot of money to the crew. It would if there weren't so many of them. But sometimes these fellows go out and suffer in terrible cold and risk their lives on the ice from March until June and come out with a nett profit of fifteen dollars! That sum is taken home for flour and molasses, tea and salt, during the months which must pass before fish money comes in. It's not always this bad. Once the *Wolf* went out and brought in 26,912 seals in eleven days. She had 255 men aboard who got 72 dollars each (£14). The biggest sum I ever heard of being distributed gave each sealing man 303 dollars for his season's work (£60). But against this the *Seal* came in not long ago, after a hard struggle and was able to give her crew only 15.57 dollars each. Many of the sweilers were married, with probably a number of children. It was inevitably a hard life for all the families".

Having got away from St. John's, the task confronting the master of a sealer was to find the "main pack", the birth place of the harp seals, where the parents and their single young one, known as "white coats", would be found in their tens of thousands. They might be anywhere on the ice north of St. John's and with no aeroplane or wireless to help him, the captain had only his instinct, his local knowledge and good lookouts in the crow's nest to rely on. Among the Newfoundlanders, who had a quaint dialect and vocabulary of their own, rather Irish in character, the captain who could find the "white coats" quickly, with consequent monetary advantage to his sweilers, was known as a Jowler.

One does not read of trouble between the ships' personnel and the sweilers, for they seem to have been a cheery and willing crowd, but Dr. Lindsay tells us of one way of dealing with trouble when it did come in the *Aurora*. A couple of days after leaving St. John's he heard a noise on deck and went up to investigate. "On the poop a lot of duffs were lying about like

64-lb. shot. A crowd of angry men could be seen on the main deck and facing them was the captain. (The captain was James Fairweather, a very well-known name in Scottish whalers, the same man who was in the *Morning* in 1914). A big Newfoundland man came up the steps and, breaking a duff in two, held it up and asked the captain to look at it. It was an awkward moment and called for immediate action. But the captain was a man of action so he planted a blow between the man's eyes and asked him to look at that, the man dropped back dazed and the trouble came to an end at once".

The end of the *Aurora* is worth recording, for when Dr. Lindsay sailed in her in 1884 no-one could have foreseen how she was to finish up. In the 90's she went under the houseflag of the famous Newfoundland firm of C. T. Bowring and remained with them as a sealer until 1911, the veteran sealing captain Abram Kean who wrote "Old and Young Ahead", having her from 1898 to 1905. In 1911 she was bought for the Australasian Antarctic Expedition and appears in Lloyd's Register up till 1917, as owned by Sir Ernest Shackleton, with J. R. Stenhouse in command. By 1917 anything that could float earned a big freight and on June 20th 1917, the *Aurora*, although quite unsuitable for such a trade, left Sydney N.S.W. with a cargo of coal for Iquique. And that was the end for her, for she never arrived. She "disappeared from human ken". The words may be hackneyed, even theatrical, but they have about them something of the dark mystery implicit in the fate of all those ships, so tragically numerous, which sailed away into oblivion in sailing ship days.

The *Esquimaux* killed 10,100 seals, but there her good fortune ended for she damaged her bow, so badly in the ice, that she had to abandon any idea of going north for the "old sealing" and whaling, and returned to Dundee after effecting temporary repairs at St. John's. They lost a member of the crew at the sealing, an elderly Shetland Islander, rather feeble, who fell through the ice and was drowned. The ship was about twenty years old at the time and her decks leaked very badly and when trimming coal in the bunkers in bad weather the men had to wear oilskins.

John Murray left the *Esquimaux* at the end of this voyage and did not sail in her again. She lasted as a whaler until the early

1900s appearing in Lloyd's Register for 1902/03 as without owner or port of registry and her subsequent career is obscure.

John Murray now "swallowed the anchor" and commenced serving his time as an engineering apprentice with a Peterhead firm. His reasons for taking this step are unknown but it may have been that even then, he realised that the whaling industry as practised in Britain was a dying one. Whatever his reasons, he did not remain an engineer for long, and following an accident to his knee went back to sea in 1890 as second mate and bosun of the brig *Alert* under his father. Like the *Perseverance* the *Alert* was a sailing vessel, without engines, and even smaller than her. She had been built at Peterhead in 1853 and had a tonnage of only 143. Her Dimensions were 82 × 21.6 × 11.3, a proportion of beams to length of about 3.7, and with her tubby hull and single topsails might have sailed right out of the 1700s. She was at this time, owned by the firm of Duthie & Co. who also owned the auxiliary whaling barque *Earl of Mar and Kelly*.

In this tiny vessel, of which John Murray spoke with affection and always referred to as "the *Alert* brig" he made a voyage to Cumberland Gulf with the stores for the trading posts owned by the Aberdeen firm of Noble. The mate, an elderly man unused to the Arctic, went out of his mind on the outward passage due to his fear of icebergs, but recovered later. The *Alert* returned to Peterhead with a cargo of whale and seal oil, sealskins and other Arctic produce and was very nearly wrecked in Montrose Bay in a howling easterly gale which caused the loss of many sailing craft. She was towed from there to Peterhead, where John left her. She lasted until 1902 when she was wrecked in Cumberland Gulf after nearly fifty years in the Arctic.

The winter of 1890/91 John put in as an A.B. in the steamers *Meredith* and *Esk* and in early 1891 joined his old ship, the sailing whaler *Perseverance*, as an A.B. for a voyage to Hudson's Bay with stores for the trading posts of Hudson's Bay Company, to whom she had been sold since John's earlier voyage in her. He joined her in Peterhead, and from there the barque proceeded to Stromness in the Orkneys to transship cargo from the auxiliary ship-rigged *Erik*, a whaler also owned by the Hudson's Bay Company. During the stay at Stromness a baker's lad called Budge used to bring down the fresh bread and on his visits expressed a wish to go away to sea. For reasons unknown the cook-steward left the ship at Stromness and replacements in that small port being scarce the baker's lad was signed-on in his place.

The *Perseverance* had been laid up in Peterhead the previous winter and all her stores including cutlery and crockery, had been put ashore. By an oversight these items were not put back aboard and the barque left Peterhead without any of these rather necessary utensils, so the afterguard had to borrow a few chipped old enamelled cups and plates from the focsle. To make matters worse, it did not take long after leaving Stromness to discover that the baker's lad, although willing enough had not even the most rudimentary ideas about cooking. Following endless complaints from both officers and men, the captain asked young Murray if he would take on the cook's job, which he did, and filled the post for some time until an old sailor called Sandy took over.

A voyage on a small sailing vessel across the North Atlantic and into Hudsons Bay could never be uneventful. In addition to the ice, through which she had to force her way for hundreds of miles unaided by an engine, it is certain that the *Perseverance*'s magnetic compass was so sluggish as to be almost useless because of the proximity of the magnetic pole; and it is equally certain that the charts being used were unreliable, due to the lack of knowledge of the region at that time. But of these hazards John Murray never mentioned a word, but had plenty to say about happenings after they got into Hudson's Bay and were approaching Fort York: "We were running in towards the land with a strong easterly wind, with a heavy sea running and drizzling rain making the visibility poor, when we suddenly started bumping—we had run onto the shoals at the north side of the Hayes River on which Fort York stands. She bumped badly and all hands gathered aft expecting some of the gear to come down from aloft, but the tide was ebbing and soon the barque was hard and fast ashore. I knew she could not come to any harm like that so I went away and turned in. Next morning at daylight I turned out and found we were aground about two miles from the land, surrounded by mud and big black boulders. Later a boat came down the river and the people in it walked across the mud to the ship. It was the doctor from the fort with some half breeds. When he left again, one of his men, George Oman, stayed with us and piloted us up the river when we were once more afloat. As we sailed slowly up river the Governor of the Hudson's Bay Company with his wife and other officials with their wives from Fort York came down the river in a boat to welcome us.

"PERSEVERANCE"

"In earlier days the arrival of a vessel at Fort York was a great event, one of the big days of the year, but I'm afraid the captain and the officers of the *Perseverance* were in no fit state to welcome anyone, being quite frankly drunk. The captain was a very likeable man and up to the time we ran ashore had been very abstemious, so I was surprised to see him 'under the influence'. The mate was staggering round half-stupefied and the second mate was no better, and I felt ashamed that the Governor should be met in such a way".

The captain asked if I would try to prepare a meal for them, so I told him: "I'll cook the food but what about the plates? You can't give it to them on those old chipped things you borrowed from us". So the meal was cancelled and all the Governor got was a bottle of beer, something he hadn't had for a long time". The *Perseverance* anchored off Fort York and it was not long before the captain had gone ashore with the Governor, apparently quite happy to leave his ship in the charge of two drunken mates. Before he went he told the crew they could have a run ashore after knock off time, and this they did, altho' not without an argument with the second mate, who was still drunk. It would seem that the second mate had been in some sort of trouble earlier, for his threat to one of the men that he would "take him ashore and flog and salt him" produced the reply that "you've had your certificate 'tapped' already for a game like that".

Discipline of any sort appears to have been temporarily laid aside aboard the *Perseverance* at that time and when John Murray and his shipmates returned from the shore that night, they found a deplorable state of affairs. The old watchman was drunk and in hoisting the boat managed to let go the for'd fall, up-ending the boat and nearly shooting the carpenter into the fast-flowing icy river. The old man told them a rambling story about the former baker's lad, who had been disrated to Ordinary Seaman when it was found that he could not cook, piling all the clothes that he could find in the focsle into a heap and then trying to set fire to the ship. But when the men went for'd they found the focsle in perfect order and no sign of the former baker's lad demoted to Ordinary Seaman. On being further questioned the old man told them that the two mates had gone for'd and dragged the lad, clad only in his underwear, along aft and after handcuffing him had put him down on top of the freshwater tanks—an action, which in the bitter cold might have caused his death.

Everyone turned in, but sleep was impossible for some time, the drunken watchman lying in his bunk howling of the days he had spent with Captain David Gray aboard the whaler *Eclipse*. The next thing John Murray knew, he was being roused by the ex-baker's lad. He was in a pitiful state, with lips swollen and bleeding and his body a mass of bruises. For a time he was unable to speak but eventually related what had happened. He had been lying in his bunk reading, with his dungaree pants shading the light, when the two mates, both crazed with drink, had entered with the watchman and dragged and kicked him along aft. It later transpired that the two mates and the watchman, who had been shipmates before, had foregathered in the cabin and drinking all available liquor had broken into the Captain's room and stolen a demijohn of whisky intended for the Governor and, as John Murray said "had a pretty good evening killing whales all over again". When they eventually came to their senses the mates realised that their acts of brutality could have serious consequences for them and were very kind to the former baker's lad, who presumably had lost all his romantic ideas about going to sea.

From Fort York (York Factory) the *Perseverance* sailed up to Fort Churchill, taking a clergyman and his wife and a little girl as passengers. The shortness of crockery since leaving Peterhead was still causing trouble, as when the old cook, Sandy, had to make porridge for the parson's little girl in a teapot and forgot to wash the tea leaves out before making it. Approaching Fort Churchill a boat was seen making for the ship. It was of a type known as a Peterhead boat, due to the fact that it had been introduced into that region by a Peterhead carpenter who had lived there for a long time. Sailing across the bows of the barque the boat fouled the head gear and was over in a second. The occupants managed to grab the gear and haul themselves aboard but all their gear, including rifles, was lost. John Murray had nothing to say about Fort Churchill, which in those days, was a very primitive place. No-one at that time could have foreseen that it would become an important grain port and railway terminus. The *Perseverance* discharged her stores, loaded Arctic produce of all kinds, and set off back to London before the winter set in. Apart from an encounter with heavy ice near Charles Island, in Hudson Straits, the voyage home was uneventful and the little barque docked in London after a fine run. A fortunate ending to a voyage which had certainly had its distasteful moments.

John Murray tells us something of this, his first visit to London, in long-ago 1891: "We were to be paid off the following day at Tower Hill, so when she was safely moored we gave her a pump out and all hands went ashore to have a look round. Another A.B. and I went to Queens Music Hall, down Poplar way and did not get out until about 1 a.m. We asked a policeman if he could direct us to somewhere to sleep and he took us to a lodging house. When they eventually let us in, we had to pay for our beds first, at a sort of pay box. The price was four pence! When the fellow at the pay box saw my watch and chain he advised me to 'put it out of sight before you go inside'. My mate said: "This is a hell of a place, let's get out of it", but I persuaded him to stay. "It might have been better if they had not stayed, for soon they found that the place was alive with bugs". Soon I lost my temper and made nasty remarks about the place and those who patronised it . . . . Threats were coming from all parts of the room and a party in the next bed objected to my remarks and offered to come over and punch my face, so I invited him over. He soon quietened now. I got up and went outside to a back yard, slipped off all my clothes, gave them a good shake and entered 'hell' once more. But I could get no sleep so called my mate and told him I was going outside to walk the streets till the public baths opened . . . We hung about till the pubs opened about 6 a.m., had a beer and a rest and then resumed our search for a public bath. We eventually found one and got rid of the bugs which had tormented us.

"I was anxious about our old cook, Sandy, for I had seen him the previous day with a couple of girls and advised him then to get himself a room for the night. I knew what would happen to him if he stayed with the girls, and I was right. We met him the next morning and he told us the sad story. As I had warned him, the girls had taken all his money and even stolen his boots. But he was lucky, for as he hobbled along the street a dock labourer took pity on him and found an old pair of boots for him. Sandy was going along to Tower Hill Shipping Office when he passed a seamens' shop kept by a Jew who invited him in to have a look round. Sandy got a fine new suit and a pair of boots and arranged to see the shopkeeper at the Shipping Office when he had been paid off. Having received his money Sandy slipped out of the back door of the Shipping Office, and found his way to the Aberdeen boat, leaving the Jew waiting for the little fat Scotsman to pay him his money. I guess he's waiting there yet! Sandy looked simple but he knew a thing or two!".

CHAPTER FIVE

THE HUDSON'S BAY COMPANY

AFTER this voyage in the *Perseverance* John Murray sat for and obtained his second mate's certificate at Aberdeen. There was one moment in the oral examination for seamanship—always something of an ordeal—when owing to having spent so long in ships fitted with a bentinck boom on the foresail, he forgot the drill when tacking a ship fitted with the normal tacks and sheets and gave a wrong answer to a seamanship question, but was able to satisfy the examiner that he knew his work. Having obtained his certificate John obtained employment as a second mate of the steam whaling barque *Hope* which had just been sold by her Peterhead owner, R. J. Kidd, to the Newfoundland firm of Grieves. She had been built at Aberdeen in 1873 by the famous firm of Hall for Captain John Gray (II) as an improvement on the *Eclipse*, which had been built in 1867 for his brother, Captain David Gray, known as "the Prince of Whalers" because of his success at the fishing. The *Hope* will always be associated with Captain John Gray (II) for he commanded her from the time she was built right up to the time she was sold to Grieves in 1891 — 18 years. He was master in the whalers for 39 years and, as if the Arctic was the only place for him, died only a year after retirement.

A spar plan of the *Hope* in Lubbock's "The Arctic Whalers" shows her with the big single topsails and topgallants which were the standard rig for whalers, although strangely enough there is a photo of her, taken at Aberdeen in 1873, in which she is shown with double topsails. In the *Hope*, John went across to St. John's N.F.L. in ballast and after picking up the sweilers set off to find the "white coats" under a sealing master called Pope. This expedition was not a very successful one for, as Captain Murray told me, "we captured only about 13,000 seals after being out at the ice for six weeks, and as there were 300 of a crew, each man's share did not amount to much". He left the *Hope* in St. John's and returned to Scotland by steamer. The *Hope* was a sealer until 1901, being wrecked on the rocks of Byron Cove, Gulf of St. Lawrence, on 31st March of that year. Her catch of 5,000 seals was lost but her crew of 194 men was rescued by the sealer *Greenland*, which it is of interest to note was almost a sister ship of the *Hope*. As an illustration of the risks run by the sealers, the *Greenland* herself was lost a few years later, on 23rd March 1907, being crushed in the ice on the Newfoundland coast, her crew being rescued by other sealers.

John was now in his twenty-fourth year, an age when he could easily have given up whaling and gone into some shipping company. The fact that he did not do so, seems to indicate that he stuck to whaling by choice. It was at this time that he met Captain Ingles, Marine Superintendent of the Hudson's Bay Company, and was given the option of going second mate in one of that company's ships, either the barque *Lady Head* or his old ship the *Perseverance*. As the *Lady Head* was only taking out stores to the company's posts in Hudson's Bay and would be back in a few months, John elected to join the *Perseverance* as it was intended that she should do a wintering whaling voyage and he wanted to put in his time for his first mate's certificate as speedily as possible. The *Lady Head* was a wooden barque of only 457 tons, built at Sunderland in 1865, and not to be confused with another barque of the same name built at Quebec in 1857 and at one time registered in Scarborough. There was another reason why John Murray wanted to join the *Perseverance*, this being that his elder brother Alex was now in command. Alex Murray had not started his sea life as a whaler, having served his time as a sailmaker in Peterhead and later sailed in that capacity aboard the full-rigged ship *Bremen* under Captain Dougal. The *Bremen* was a big iron ship built for the North German Lloyd as a steamer back in 1858 and converted to Sail in the 70's.

The year was now 1892 and Scottish whaling was in a poor state due to the extermination of the right whale. Because of the scarcity of 'fish' it was decided to send the *Perseverance* to try out

a whaling ground entirely new to Scottish whalers. This was in
the northern part of Hudson's Bay, to the west of Southampton
Island, in about 65 north 87 west. Leaving Peterhead at the
beginning of June 1892 the *Perseverance*arrived off the mouth
of Hudson Strait about a month later. As it was decided to
augment the crew with Eskimos there were only about fifteen
men in the focsle where normally there would have been twice
that number. The passage through Hudson Strait was very
slow due to great quantities of ice and at the end of July the
barque was off Ashe Inlet, on Big Island, towards the western
end of Hudson Strait. A fortnight later, land was sighted which
was identified as Cape Fullerton, at the western entrance to
Roes Welcome, the stretch of water separating Southampton
Island from the mainland.John remarked that "as no-one on
board the ship had ever been in the northern part of Hudson's
Bay before, and the charts in many parts only gave a brief
outline of the land, we had to feel our way round. We kept on,
feeling our way up Roes Welcome and experiencing fog almost
every day". This was seafaring of a type little different to that
practised in the days of Captain Luke Foxe, who in 1631 had
discovered Roes Welcome while searching for the elusive
North-West Passage to China. Since his day, there have been
many expeditions to the north, each adding its quota of
knowledge, but even so, the fogs were just as dense, the cold
just as numbing and the compass little more reliable than in
Foxe's day. In Hudson Strait there is close on fifty degrees of
magnetic variation, and the note "magnetic disturbance" is
frequently found on charts of the area; and even today, ninety
years after John Murray was there in the *Perseverance* there
are still stretches of coast in the area outlined in dots to show
they have never been surveyed.

In spite of all her difficulties, the *Perseverance* worked her
way up Roes Welcome until she was north of Wager Inlet,
discovered in 1742 by Captain Middleton, when a whale boat
was sighted making for the ship. It contained several Eskimos,
with their wives and children, returning from a deer-hunting
expedition, and the men were immediately engaged by Captain
Alex Murray to assist in whaling. They were Iviliks, a tribe
whose habitat was round about Repulse Bay and Roes

Welcome who were good deer hunters and boatmen and had already been employed by the American whalers which for some years had found their way up there. The *Perseverance* finally anchored at the head of Repulse Bay, a large inlet on the mainland north-west of Southampton Island with which is associated the names of several men famous in Arctic exploration. Middleton discovered it in 1742, and in 1821 Parry examined it more closely and confirmed Middleton's statement that it was merely an inlet and not the long-sought North-West Passage. Dr. Rae in 1846 and the American Captain Hall in the 1860's were others who knew Repulse Bay. Today there are trading posts and a Catholic Mission, but when John Murray was there in the *Perseverance* it was exactly as it had been when Middleton first visited it one hundred and fifty years earlier. Having anchored, Captain Alex Murray went off with two boats to find a suitable harbour for the barque while her boats were hunting for whales. He returned in a couple of days and the vessel was shifted down to a berth among a group of small islands known as the Kekertens. This title is rather confusing as a proper name, for 'Kekerten' is an Eskimo word meaning island and there are at least two other groups so named: in Franklin Strait and in Cumberland Sound.

The *Perseverance* lay at anchor among the islands for the remainder of the short summer while her boats left the ship at daylight each morning and cruised round on the lookout for whales. Several were seen but appeared to be very shy, probably due to the shoal water. Two whales were, however, captured and when the first ice formed on October 1st and finished the whaling for that season they had the satisfaction of knowing that whatever their luck might be later, they would not return to Peterhead a "clean ship". When the ice was about six inches thick the anchor was hove up, a dock was cut out for the ship, she was moored with her head to the north and frozen in that position. Then a snow wall was built round the vessel, about two feet from her sides and the intervening space filled up with soft snow right up to the main deck. The Eskimos helped in this work and also cut out blocks of frozen snow with which the decks were covered, this being done to prevent the decks from splitting in the intense cold. The whale boats were hauled out on the ice and turned bottom-up after being filled with snow and when all this had been done the ship was ready to face a northern winter. Externally, she appeared as three masts sticking up out of the snow.

Once the winter had set in, there was little real work to keep the crew occupied. They were given such jobs as making mats for thole pins in the boats and sennit for dog traces, or cutting fresh water ice and setting traps for foxes. Regarding foxes at this time, John Murray made the rather surprising remark that "fox furs being of little value, the traps were put out more for exercising the crew than anything else". Some of the men took up with Eskimo women and had them living aboard with them, the captain choosing to shut his eyes to this irregularity. Many Eskimos visited the ship, among them members of the Nitchilik tribe, which lived on King William Island, not far from the magnetic pole. These natives were the best sealers. From the Eskimos it was learned that two American whalers, the *A.R. Tucker* and the *Canton* had wintered nearby the previous year.

Some time before the New Year the Eskimos were told that they were to be given a big dinner on that day, and from then on any natives who were going off deer-hunting always asked how many "sleeps" to the big day, so they could be back in time for it. For days before the big event, the cook was busy making plum puddings and on the last day of the old year the tweendecks were cleared out for the big dance. Unlike the natives of Cumberland Sound, who had known the Scottish whalers for many years and had picked up their customs, the natives of Repulse Bay had never seen a foursome reel nor heard a melodeon, but it did not take them long to pick up the dance and once having started the trouble was to get them to stop, for they were quite tireless. When at midnight the ship's bell was rung and everyone went round shaking hands, they were very bewildered, until it was explained to them that "happy new year" meant "plenty seals, no hunger, no sickness". After that, they went round shaking hands all over again and trying to pronounce "happy new year".

Almost without exception throughout the history of their association with Europeans the Eskimos have shown themselves to be a cheerful, kindly and hospitable people and

Captain Murray had nothing but good to say of them. Even so, their attitude towards death might seem callous to some Europeans, although in reality it was based on the struggle for existence which went on all their lives. In the nearly fifty years he knew the Innuits, Captain Murray saw many examples of the impassive attitude towards death and there was an example of it that winter in the *Perseverance*. An old Eskimo, feeling that he was an encumbrance to his sons now that he was no longer able to go hunting, had them suspend a thong from the roof of his igloo with a loop on the end of it. Putting his head through the loop, he put all his weight on it and strangled himself by sheer willpower. Once dead, little reverence was shown for the departed and the old man's sons took the corpse over to a nearby island and, covering it with snow, left it. John Murray tells us that "a week or so later one of the boat-steerers and I were taking a walk round a line of traps we had set, when we found the old man's corpse partly uncovered and the face eaten away by a wolverine. We tied a thong round his feet and set off to drag him down into the valley where we could find some loose stones and bury him properly. On the way the old man took charge and went rolling down the hill, making a noise like a bouncing ball as he went over the bumps. Eventually we got him down and I then sent for the two sons to come and bring crowbars with which to loosen the frozen earth to make a grave. I noticed that when they arrived they took off their outer clothing before they would handle the body".

During the winter, John spent a lot of his time with the Eskimos hunting deer, and when the spring at last returned, kept the ship and the natives supplied with caribou meat. The place at which the *Perseverance* wintered, was on the track of the caribou making their spring migration to the north and any number could have been killed; but with the weather getting warmer and no means of preserving the meat, only enough for the immediate needs was shot.

At the beginning of May (1893), the ship's six whaleboats were taken by sledge to Beach Point, at the entrance to Repulse Bay, and stationed there to keep a lookout for whales. They were there about a month, a cold and cheerless time which was entirely unproductive, for although a few whales were seen, they never had a chance to get near them — the noise of the boat going through the young ice which formed every night scared the whales long before one could get near them. Only men in perfect physical condition could have endured the conditions prevailing at Beach Point. Captain Murray, not a man to make much of hardships, tells us: "the weather was very cold when the wind was in the north, the thermometer sometimes dropping below zero. It was fearfully cold sleeping in the boats with only a canvas cover over them. We had no primus stove, and to make our coffee, had to build a snow wall in the lee of which we had our 'conjuror', a contraption something like a bucket with holes in the sides which burned wood and blubber. About the end of May, orders were sent down for me to take the three boats, each with a months provisions, and go down to Whale Point, in Roes Welcome, and stay there until the ship arrived in August. Provisions would be sent to me every month. One of the boats was manned entirely by Eskimos, the other boat and my own each having a white harpooner. It was not an easy job to get down to Whale Point, because of the ice. Sometimes the tides moved the land ice out sufficiently for us to make a few miles sailing and rowing, but more often we had to get our harness on and pull the boats over the ice. With them full of whaling gear and provisions, it was hard going and of a night we needed no rocking to get to sleep, being tired out. The most dangerous part of the trip was in crossing Wager Inlet, where the currents ran as much as seven or eight knots and move the pack ice up and down. Our only chance of getting across was at the turn of the tide, when for a short time it was slack water. I stood on a hummock of ice keeping a lookout and as soon as I saw the tide easing up, shouted to the others to make a dash for it. The older of the two harpooners shouted that he would not try it: 'I'm not going through that lot' he declared; 'If I do, we'll lose the boat and half the crew'. "Come on now" I urged him, "there's no time to wait. If you don't you'll find yourself up at the head of Wager Inlet in a few hours". I managed to get through and reached the water on the south side, and the other boats followed me, the old white harpooner just managing to get across before the ice closed in. Eventually we reached the land near Whale Point and hauled our boats up and lay there for about three weeks, unable to do any whaling because of the ice. We had several visits from the Angouts, the medicine men of the Eskimos, who went down to the edge of the ice and prayed for the pack ice to move off so the boats could get afloat. Finally it did move and we had quite a broad lane of water. About this time three American whale boats, full of Eskimos, arrived from Cape Fullerton and I felt ashamed when I saw how much better they were than our clumsy heavy boats. As regards the whaling gear, too, I felt we were about fifty years behind the times". The sole object of this voyage was the capture of whales, and when one reflects the real hardships and dangers endured by the crew of the *Perseverance* one cannot avoid the thought: was it worth it?

John Murray goes on to tell us:"Our stores were now about exhausted and we began looking anxiously for the boat coming up Repulse Bay with more. It turned up in July and a bitter disappointment awaited us. The boat was an old leaky American one and they had been a month on the way, sealing all the time, with the result that the stores were uneatable, being saturated with blood and grease. The biscuit was in sacks, and the Eskimos had been sleeping on them and jumping up and down on them so that they were ground up into powder. The container for the sugar was leaky and there was practically none left. "For some time now our food has consisted of seal and walrus meat, but fortunately one of the American boats manned by Eskimos got a small whale, so we had plenty of whale meat and mucktuk (the skin of the whale) which makes very good eating if you have the appetite. We longed for a piece of hard bread (biscuit) as we had had none for over two months. Meat and coffee, with nothing else, don't go well together. Another thing we were short of was tobacco".

In July, John took his boats to a little bay on the north side of Whale Point, he and the two white harpooners living in one tupik and the Eskimos in others. One day they had a visit from some Kinipatu natives, who live around Chesterfield Inlet. One of them was a dark skinned man who announced himself as William Williebuck and told John in good English that he had worked for the Hudson's Bay Company for many years. He stayed talking to John for some time and before leaving asked him if he would care for some eider duck eggs. John told him: "I haven't much to give you, but bring your eggs along and we'll have a look at them". Willie brought along two big cans of eggs and after talking some more I told him to leave them and I'd try to find something to give him for them. After he had gone I said to my Eskimo boat-steerer: 'Jask, take these two pails of eggs and try them in that pool of water behind the tupik. Those that float, put into one pail, those that sink in the other, and bring them back here'. It turned out that the eggs were about fifty per cent floaters and fifty per cent sinkers, and when Williebuck came back I told him it would be selfish for us to keep all the eggs and gave him back the pail of floaters, being quite sure that to an Eskimo it made no difference whether the eggs were good or bad".

In the second half of July and in August, Roes Welcome was about clear and they managed to secure two whales before the *Perseverance* arrived off Whale Point on 22nd August. There were some American whalers in the area at this time, the barques *Canton* and *A. R. Tucker* and the schooner *Era*. They were all old ships whose oil-soaked timbers could have told many a story of adventure and tragedy if they could have spoken. The *Canton* had been built at Swansea, South Wales, in 1835, the *A. R. Tucker* at Dartmouth in 1851 and the *Era* at Boston in 1847, The *Canton* was the first to arrive and John Murray tells us: "About the middle of August an American whaler, the *Canton*, arrived and hove-to with her main tops'l aback about two miles south of the Point. We sent a boat across to her and borrowed four buckets of hard bread which were to be paid back on the arrival of our own vessel. While I was aboard her, they lowered a boat and put into it the body of a sailor who had died the day before. That was the third sailor who had died since they left home a month earlier. One evening our crew were having a dance on deck when the captain of the *Canton*, Fisher by name, paid a visit to our captain and I heard him say to my brother: 'How many of your men died last winter, cap'n?' My brother replied: 'Not one. There has not been a headache among the lot', at which the

American gloomily remarked: 'Good God, I'll be thankful if I can take the half of my crew home; I buried the third one a few days ago'.

"We were cruising round one day on the lookout for days in the company of an American ship and I could see two sailors perched up aloft in the rings. Later I heard that these men had been given three days aloft as a punishment for stealing a few handfuls of sugar while working among the stores on deck". There were several radical differences in the way things were run aboard Scottish and New England whalers. Undoubtedly the biggest as regards the actual whaling was that when an American whaler killed a fish it was "tried out" on the spot, the blubber being rendered down into oil immediately. Scottish whalers never at any time did this, merely stripping the blubber off the whale and storing it in tanks aboard the ship, to be dealt with ashore at the end of the voyage. This difference in the technique of extracting the whale oil resulting in completely different operational methods. The American whaler was a self-contained unit and could stay away indefinitely, until the killing of the whale which made her a "full ship". Consequently, American whalers would often stay away for years, roaming the seas of the world in search of the elusive sperm whale, and not always returning home when they had at last filled up, for sometimes they would discharge their oil in some port far from home and set off on another cruise. Operated in such a way, the crews of American whalers were invariably a very mixed crowd, generally including some Cape Verde Islanders but having the balance of the men who, if they were seamen at all, knew nothing about whaling. When a whaler needed a crew, an advertisement was sometimes put in the newspapers, enlarging on the delights of a whaling cruise, and John Murray spoke of one occasion when a reporter from the Boston "Globe", lured by such an advertisement and thinking he could make a good story out of a trip in a "blubber hunter", joined the ship with a fine rifle as part of his equipment, only to have it taken away from him as soon as the vessel got away to sea. In John R. Spears's book "The Story of the New England Whalers" he gives the case of a Washington reporter who thought to see the world from the deck of a whaler.

"You think we'll do?" the man asked timidly of the crimp who had offered to get them a berth. "Oh, no doubt about it", replied the crimp. "I'm willing to risk you, though I may lose something by it. If you are *determined* to make a voyage, I'll put you in the way of shipping in a most elegant vessel, well-fitted — the *Vigilana*, and activity will ensure your rapid promotion. I haven't the least doubt but you will come home boat steerers. I sent off six college students a few days ago, and a poor fellow who had been flogged away from home by a vicious wife. A whaler, gentlemen — a whaler is a place of refuge for the dissipated, an asylum for the needy. There's nothing like it. You can see the world — you can see something of life".

The American New England whalers were indeed "tramps", but not so the Scottish whalers. Speaking of the period covering Captain Murray's sea career, they confined their activities solely to the Arctic seas and unless they made a wintering voyage such as the *Perseverance* was doing, left their home port in the early spring and returned at the freeze-up in the autumn. It seems probable that the only occasion any of them ever crossed the equator was on that unfortunate voyage in 1892/93 when four of them went to the Antarctic in search of "right" whales and returned without seeing a single one.

The seasonal nature and short voyages of Scottish whalers attracted a class of seaman who, living in the ship's home port, sailed in them year after year. This made for a happier atmosphere aboard them, than that prevailing in the majority of New England ships with their crews of pick-ups often speaking different languages. It was important to have harpooners and boat steerers who knew the whaling business, but the deckhands were not so important. Towards the end of Scottish whaling, when it had become a very chancey business because of the disappearance of the "right" whale, it would seem that the quality of the men who went to the whaling declined, and as will be seen, trouble with them not altogether unknown.

Another point of difference between Scottish and New England craft was that the former were mostly fitted with engines while few Americans were. Right up to the end of American whaling of the old type, which was in 1925, when the old barque *Wanderer* was wrecked on the Massachusetts coast, the New England craft remained engineless. Other minor differences were that Scottish whale boats were much heavier than American ones. There was, however, a reason for this in that Scottish boats were built especially for work in the ice where American ones were used far more in temperate and tropical waters. American whale line was much lighter than that used in the Scottish whalers, which was a heavier steam-tarred line that would sink under the ice more readily — an advantage. On the other hand, American line coiled much more easily than the steam-tarred type.

There was another suicide among the Eskimos that summer, again that of an old man who considered himself an encumbrance to his sons. Going some distance from the settlement he built himself a grave of stones and lay down in it, intending to starve himself to death. But when, after two days, he had not lapsed into the unconsciousness he had hoped for, he became so hungry that he got up and returned to the settlement for some food. Later he returned to his grave and again lay down, but this time made sure of the release he sought by cutting veins in both his wrists, so that he quickly bled to death.

After the *Perseverance* had came down from Repulse Bay she cruised in the vicinity of Whale Point until the approach of winter, but without killing a single whale. Captain Alex Murray then paid off his Eskimos and took the barque back to Peterhead. She had caught four whales during her long spell in the Arctic and among other Arctic produce had 235 seal skins, valued at approximately seven shillings per skin.

Not discouraged by the results of the wintering voyage the Hudson's Bay Company sent the *Perseverance* out again the following year, again with the intention of making it a wintering voyage. John Murray had obtained his first mate's certificate while at home and this voyage sailed as mate. His elder brother was still in command and as the voyage was to be a long one his wife accompanied him. They left Peterhead about the middle of June (1894) and on the 27th July sighted Resolution Island, lying at the entrance to Hudson Strait, and on that day met the pack ice. They managed to get into Hudson Strait by keeping well clear of Cape Chidley and made good progress through loose ice. The boats were now all swung out ready to go after a whale if one was sighted but none were seen. On 30th July the barque was off Big Island, in Hudson Strait, but the progress was very slow after that and it took 17 days to cover the 500 miles from there to Cape Fullerton, in Ne Altra Strait, at the entrance to Roes Welcome. This averages about thirty miles a day and one wonders how young Mrs. Murray took to this life, a hard one for men long used to the conditions of Arctic seafaring.

John tells us of the reception Mrs. Murray got from Eskimo women who had never seen a white woman before: "August 17th, vessel was off Cape Fullerton and soon we had two boat crews of Eskimos on board. The news soon spread that we had the captain's wife aboard, and the following day, while cruising off Whale Point in the company of two American whalers we had a visit in the evening from quite a number of Eskimo women, who were all anxious to see Mrs. Murray. The women stood on deck in groups peering along towards the cabin but too shy to go down there. Mrs. Murray was watching them through a porthole, too shy herself to go on deck. After some time one of the women, more daring than the rest, went into the cabin and soon it was full of Eskimo women, Mrs. Murray coming out of her room and shaking hands with all of them. The women were of course very interested in Mrs. Murray's clothes, particularly with the then fashionable balloon sleeves on her dress. The following evening, it being fine, we had just about all the women from Whale Point aboard. They must have been working overtime, I think, for they were all wearing the balloon sleeves they had seen on Mrs. Murray's dress, on their print dresses, except for one woman who had made her dress out of bath towels with the fringes hanging down".

The summer was a complete failure for the *Perseverance* as far as whaling was concerned. A whale was seen on 27th August but when winter closed down and put an end to any more whaling she was a clean ship. In early September she was sailed down to Depot Island, on the southern side of the entrance to Chesterfield Inlet, where it was intended to winter, the exact position being three miles west of the island. There are, incidentally, two other islands of the same name, both of them far to the north of Chesterfield Inlet. About 5th September, the two American whaling barques *A. R. Tucker*–Captain West, and *Canton*–Captain Fisher, lay off the island with their mainsails and topsails aback and paid a visit. They reported the *A. R. Tucker* with four whales, the *Canton* with five. From then on until the ice formed, there was a succession of strong easterly gales which stopped all whaling. It must have been a worrying time for the captain with his young wife aboard, for on one occasion, with the barque diving her bows right under as she rode out a screaming gale, he had to give consideration to running her ashore as the only hope of saving their lives. Fortunately the chains held and she rode it out, but all hands were thankful when at last the ice formed and they were frozen-in.

Much the same procedure was carried out to make the ship secure and comfortable as had been done the previous year but this time a large tent made out of sails was erected on the ice and was used as a workshop for repairing the boats and also for dancing and trials of strength between the Eskimos. They sometimes gave a performance called the "clouty", which was carried out as follows: the instrument used for this was a hoop about two feet in diameter, covered with parchment and fitted with a handle. It was held in the left hand while in the right, the performer had an wooden instrument something like a potato masher with which he struck the rim of the hoop, producing a boom-boom sound. In effect, it was a type of drum. The Eskimo women sat round in a circle and sang a song in time with the boom of the drum, and on occasion the performer on the "clouty" would keep it up until he was foaming at the mouth and fell exhausted on the ground.

The Eskimos sometimes held contests between the young men of different tribes, mostly the Iviliks and Nichiliks. One form of bout was for two young men to face each other, stripped to the waist, and for one of them to start by presenting the side of his face to the other, who would give it a light tap with his clenched fist. The first one would return it and they would strike alternately, each blow getting harder until they were striking each other with all their force, the winner being the one who could stand it the longest. It was a brutal form of sport, and a dangerous one, as John Murray tells us: "I knew of a case where two men were pitted against each other, one a strong man from the Nichilik tribe, the other an Ivilik. They gave each other some very severe blows on the temple and at last the Nichilik had to give in, the Ivilik being hailed as the winner. But a few weeks later, the Nichilik died as a result of the fight. Strange to say, they never seemed to lose their tempers, each one taking his blow in turn. I know I could not have stood it for long. I stopped all the natives I had engaged from playing this game, as I am sure it was bad for their eyesight". A variation of this type of contest, was for the two young men to face each other and start by tapping each other on the biceps, each blow getting harder until they were hitting each other as hard as they possibly could. Of this type of contest John Murray said: "I have seen their breasts black and yellow right across and the arms swollen up to almost double their normal size. That was another game I had to put a stop to, for I wanted the men in good condition to pull an oar. I didn't mind so much during the winter, but when it came near the spring I had to stop it. The natives seem to have a great control of their tempers.

On 5th December the Eskimos seemed to be in a strangely restless mood and in the evening disappeared ashore, giving no hint as to their intentions. The next day it came out that a devil had been seen and they had gone ashore to hunt him. One man, Chukta by name, had seen the devil and got close enough to stab him with a pointed stick and showed the blood-stained stick as proof. It was known that no animal had been killed for some time and the other Eskimos were quite satisfied that Chukta had wounded the devil, Tung Nung, and that they would not be troubled again by him for a long time. Chukta was quite the hero for a few days and received a present from each of the others.

The deer were very scarce this year but in spite of it the Eskimos were very improvident and wasteful when they had plenty for their immediate needs. The result was that later in the winter they had to be fed entirely by the ship, a policy which was not solely altruistic, for as John Murray remarked: "they would have been in a very bad condition for sealing and whaling if we had not fed them".

Christmas and the New Year (1895) passed much as they had done the previous wintering voyage, with the Eskimos coming from long distances to join in the feasting and dancing. "When Christmas arrived we gave them a pretty good dinner", John Murray recorded, "and the ship's crew was treated to venison pie with a few glasses of grog to enjoy themselves. New Year's Day the natives were given a good dinner and we had some of them dressed up in white coats and tall hats, serving out the soup. They went around serving with a dignified look and obviously felt the occasion to be one of great importance. The 'tweendecks were cleaned out for the big dance to be held there after the dinner was over. Our own crew was treated to a bottle of grog each, which they soon got to the bottom of, with the result that there were sore heads the next morning. As a headache cure, the captain gave them half a bottle each".

One day that winter, Captain Alex Murray and his wife went for a walk on the ice, the captain carrying a shotgun as he hoped for a shot at a hare as they got near the land. As they approached it, they saw a polar bear galloping towards them and Captain Murray told his wife to run back to the ship while he waited to give the bear a charge of small shot in the hope that it would be scared away. Mrs. Murray would not go without him, so they both started running towards the ship, but she quickly tired and had to stop at intervals. The bear made no attempt to attack them and they reached the ship safely and later came to the conclusion that it was not chasing them at all, but had approached out of curiosity. There was a track of a sledge leading to the ship and the bear, afraid to cross it, had merely been following it to the ship. But after this experience, Mrs. Murray would not go for a walk on the ice unless her husband had a rifle with him. Probably no man who ever lived was better acquainted with polar bears than John Murray. He told me that from first to last, he killed 103 with his own rifle and thought it probably a record, as it no doubt was, and probably still is. Polar bears are insatiably inquisitive but not normally particularly savage. John gave it as his opinion that 90% of them would not attack a human being unless driven to it by hunger.

It was during this winter that John Murray saw the only case of scurvy he encountered in all his years in the Arctic. One of the seamen, very loath to take more exercise than he had to, was warned of the dangers of inactivity but took no heed and contracted scurvy in his leg. John was in a position to speak with authority on the subject of health in the Arctic and gave it as his opinion that under normal conditions any case of scurvy was due to a man's own negligence. There was also a death among the Peterhead crew that winter, a harpooner who died on 18th March. He was an elderly man who was sick for some time and died of heart trouble — a rather loose description of his ailment but the best that could be given. The Angouts ordered the other Eskimos to observe three days mourning during which they could not go sealing or fire a gun, and this order was strictly obeyed — a reverence for the dead they did not show to their own people. The coffin was taken over to Depot Island and buried in a cairn of stones at the highest point, the entire crew and many of the Eskimos attending the funeral. The following year John visited the grave and found that someone had removed a section of the coffin lid to see the old man's face, an act of desecration which was certainly not committed by the Eskimos, who despite their practical attitude towards dying had a superstitious fear of the dead. John assumed that it was someone from one of the whalers who had done it. He found the body in a wonderful state of preservation and had the coffin repaired and well-covered with stones.

On 24th April the whale boats were sent down to the floe edge but with the young ice still forming it was useless putting them in the water so, as John said: "We had nothing to do but eat, sleep, play cards and an occasional game of dominoes, which game the Eskimos liked best. When playing it, each man had to put an article of some sort on the table and sometimes would put down one of his garters, or a knife, and I once saw a man put a whaleboot down as his contribution. The winner had to pick up all the articles put down, until all had gone. They appeared to be like the Chinese, very fond of gambling". When the pack ice had at last cleared away from the land they started cruising for whales and on May 12th succeeded in killing their first one. Later John and one of the harpooners went down to Whale Point and killed two more.

There was a big event aboard the *Perseverance* in early June, when Mrs. Murray gave birth to a son without the help of a doctor, midwife or nurse. The tiny barque aboard of which the child first saw the light was never called by her full name among those who knew her but was always referred to as the "Percy" and this was the name bestowed upon the child when he came to be christened at Fort Churchill.

Arrangements were that the *Perseverance* should go to Fort Churchill to rendezvous with the steam whaling barque *Erik* and obtain stores from her which would enable her to stay in the Arctic, and on 1st August she left Whale Point, the second mate remaining there to carry on floe-edge whaling while she was away. The distance from Whale Point to Fort Churchill is only about 450 miles, but with light head winds all the way, it took her nine days. John Murray remarks in the notes he kept that "we were very sorry to leave Whale Point, for the best time for whaling was just coming on, and we were missing it through having to go for stores". Up to this time a total of four whales had been killed.

A couple of days after arriving at Fort Churchill the Hudson's Bay Company's ketch *Princess* arrived from London and on the same day the Fort Churchill chaplain, Mr. Leckhouse and Dr. Milne, Governor of Fort York came aboard.

One day, while lying at anchor waiting for the *Erik*, John spotted a wolf in the bush, so grabbing his rifle he jumped into the dinghy and went ashore to see if he could kill it. He lost track of the wolf in the bush but found something else— mosquitoes and sand flies by the million, so that by the time he got back to his boat he could hardly see. He managed to get back aboard but was practically blind for nine days.

The *Erik* eventually arrived on the 22nd August and after the *Perseverance* had put all her Arctic produce aboard her and received in exchange the stores which would enable her to stay in the Arctic another winter, Mrs. Murray and her baby and John Murray joined the *Erik* for passage to London. The mate of the *Erik* had died on the outward passage so John Murray occupied that position on the homeward voyage, although as a result of his trip after the wolf he had to keep to his room for some time, so severely had he been bitten.

The *Erik*, a small enough vessel by modern standards, was still a big ship, compared with the tiny *Perseverance*. She had been built at Dundee in 1865 by Alexander Stephens and had a gross tonnage of 533 compared with the *Perseverance*'s 179. The *Esquimaux*, in which John Murray had earlier sailed as an AB was a sister ship, as was also the *Arctic I*.

On 26th August the *Erik* towed the *Perseverance* and the ketch *Princess* well clear of the land and then cast them off to proceed on their own. The *Perseverance* headed back up north again for another lonely winter while the *Princess* sailed south to Fort York. The *Erik* set off for home via various Hudson's Bay Company's posts, the first being Fort Chimo, on the Koksoak River, in Ungava Bay. She arrived there on 7th September, a passage of 12 days for a distance of about 1000 miles, and stayed there for a fortnight, discharging cargo and loading furs and a quantity of pickled salmon trout. From there, she went on to nearby George's River, further east, where there is another Hudson's Bay Company's post, and then on to Port Burwell, just inside Cape Chidley, the eastern prong of Ungava Bay. There is a good photo of Port Burwell in the Arctic Pilot Vol. III, showing a barquentine moored up in the inner harbour with big icebergs in the foreground of the picture, and from this, one can get an idea of the difficulties facing the masters of vessels like the *Erik*. It was a type of seafaring completely different from that required in ships in temperate zones, calling for local knowledge and the ability to cope with unexpected dangers.

Murray tells us that after Port Burwell: "our next visit was to Nachoach, 'on the Labrador', (just below Cape Chidley) then on to several small ports on the way down and at last to Cartwright, where we landed some of our salmon and made preparations for the passage home to London, where we arrived about the end of October 1895. Tied up in the West India Dock and I stayed with the ship until she was discharged. So endeth the voyage".

CHAPTER SIX

FIRST COMMAND

THE following year (1896) John Murray, now possessing his master's certificate, signed an agreement with the Hudson's Bay Company to go out to Hudson's Bay and take over command of the *Perseverance* from his brother. He joined the *Erik* in London in June as third mate and took out with him a relief crew for the *Perseverance*. The master of the *Erik* at this time, was Captain Alexander Gray, a son of Captain John Gray, Senior, and a brother of Captain David Gray, known as the "Prince of Whalers". The *Erik* had a hard passage across the Atlantic, with much north-westerly wind and on 10th July saw many icebergs. Next day she was in pack ice but managed to reach Cartwright on the 12th. After that, it was her previous homeward passage in reverse and calls were made at Rigolette, Nor'west River, Davis Inlet and Nachvach, where the company's representative, Mr. Ford, and his sons boarded the ship. From there she rounded Cape Chidley and entered Hudson Straits, and had an easy passage of it from there to Fort Churchill, with little ice.

The date of arrival at Fort Churchill was 7th August and on the 13th, the *Perseverance* arrived and hauled alongside the *Erik* to transfer her Arctic produce and take on stores. On the 17th, John Murray took over command of the *Perseverance* from his brother Alex, and without any loss of time the *Erik* towed out the engineless *Perseverance* well clear of the harbour and cast off the tow line. After that, the *Perseverance* set off back to Roes Welcome and an area which by now was becoming familiar ground to Captain Murray.

On 22nd August the barque was off Cape Fullerton with two American whalers in sight and on the 24th a number of empty barrels were landed at Whale Point as it was intended to whale there the following Spring. A head of whalebone, from a fish killed while the *Perseverance* was at Fort Churchill was also taken aboard. On August 26th, the ship received a visit from Captain West of the *A. R. Tucker* who reported the schooner *Era* with two "fish", the barque *Canton* (Captain Poole) with two, and his own ship with none. He could not give any information about two other American whaling barques in the vicinity. On 26th August, the *Perseverance* took aboard some Eskimos from Whale Point and sailed for Repulse Bay.

Regarding Whale Point, the Arctic Pilot makes the following remarks: "It was an important position in the days when the whaling industry flourished. According to Captain Comer, more whales have been killed within sight of Whale Point, than in all the rest of Hudson Bay. There was, in 1904, a small house on the summit of the point, used as a look-out station by the whalers. It was also referred to as a favourite camping ground for the Eskimos in the early summer, whales, seals and walrus being then plentiful in the adjoining waters, and caribou numerous within a short distance of the coast".

The *Perseverance* made poor progress up the 'Welcome' due to strong north-easterly winds. At 5 a.m. on 3rd September, when about twenty miles north of Wager Inlet, three whaleboats were sighted making for the ship, and then a barque was seen stranded on a reef inshore. When the boats reached the *Perseverance* the first man to step aboard introduced himself as Captain Miller of the whaling barque *Desdemona*.

"There she is, capt'n", he said, indicating the wreck. "She's on a reef and never likely to come off it so I've got to find some way of getting my crew home. Can you help me?"

Captain Murray, only a few days in command of his first ship, had to make a quick decision, as to what was the best thing to do. There were two alternatives. He could either carry on to Repulse Bay, about fifty miles ahead, where he intended to winter and where he knew the American barque *Platina* was also going to winter; or he could turn south again in the hope of catching one of the two American barques he knew were down there before they left for home. "Well, captain", he said, "I'm here, and I'll help you as best as I can. I think you can make the passage down the coast in your own boats, but the difficulty is, the other ships might have sailed before you get there. If that happened, you'd have to work your way up the 'Welcome' again to get to Repulse Bay and winter there. I'll take a chance and we'll turn back, and see if we can find one of your ships to take you home. If we miss them, I'm willing to take half your men for the winter if the *Platina* will take the other half''.

This plan having been decided on, it was put into operation immediately. Lowering his own boats and manning them with Eskimos, with the second mate in charge, Captain Murray sent them off to the wreck to salvage as much whaling gear and personal effects as possible.

"You'll find all the whaling gear without any trouble", Captain Miller said, "for it is all in barrels clearly marked. There's a lot of my own gear there too. There's my sextant and two chronometers and all my navigation books and charts". He also mentioned a gold albert watch which would be found in a certain drawer and which he would like Captain Murray to have.

The second mate having left for the wreck, the three American boats were hoisted on board and the *Perseverance* set off back down Roe's Welcome. Time was now an important factor and Captain Murray, confident of the strength of his ship, drove her hard, disregarding the ice which was in large quantities on the water. "I guess we had some pretty hard bumps that night" he said, "it nearly frightened the life out of some of the *Desdemona*'s crowd, for they hadn't been used to bumping their ship the same way as we do. Their ships aren't built to stand the ice like ours are, anyhow. The following day we sighted smoke coming from the *A. R. Tucker* trying out a whale and were mighty glad to know the ships had not sailed for home, as were the shipwrecked men of the *Desdemona*.

After distributing the *Desdemona*'s men among the barques *A. R. Tucker*, *Canton* and the schooner *Era* the question arose as to the disposal of the *Desdemona*'s boats. Captain Miller wanted to keep them, but arguing that he lost valuable whaling time in returning south, Captain Murray maintained that he should keep them, and this was agreed to. The *Perseverance* then set out to thrash her way up to Roe's Welcome again. On 12th September she arrived back at the scene of the wreck and picked up the second mate and the boats. A sorry story of ineptitude then came to light.

The second mate reported that he had saved a little—a few tins of popcorn and other useless things, and when asked why, said that a small keg of white rum had been found and he was frightened to leave it, for fear that the Eskimos drank it.

Captain Murray was angry. "Why the hell didn't you put a hatchet through it and empty it and get on with your job?" he asked. "And where's the gold albert Captain Miller mentioned?" The second mate hesitated and then said he had found no gold albert. "Maybe you don't know what a gold albert is? It's a watch chain". The second mate expressed surprise and said: "Yes, I did find a watch chain but I didn't think it was of any account", and pulled out the "gold albert" wrapped up in a piece of tissue paper.

"You're goddam careful with a 'no-account' watch chain", said the irate captain, taking it from him. Further cause for anger was the second mate's treatment of the two chronometers, for he had taken them ashore and left them lying in the open, uncovered, so that they were ruined. The Eskimos had done better and saved quite a lot of 'bread' (biscuit).

If the other American whalers encountered by Captain Murray in the Arctic were old-timers, the *Desdemona* beat them all for longevity. She had been built at Middleton, Connecticut, in 1823 and restored in 1846, and so was over seventy years old, when she was finally wrecked. Her nett tonnage was only 237 and her dimensions, 99×27×15,giving her a proportion of beams to length about 3·7, made her even more tubby than the *Perseverance*. She had for many years been one of the whaling fleet of Aiken and Swift of New Bedford but at the time of her loss was owned by Thomas Luce of New Bedford. She had been laid up for a long time before her last voyage and had been entirely re-rigged, but when wrecked had not caught a single whale.

On the morning of 13th September the *Perseverance* anchored near the American whaling barque *Platina*,Captain Mackenzie. Prospects for whaling in the short time left before the freeze-up seemed good, for whales were sighted on several days but were generally too shy to let the boats get within firing distance. On the 17th, they had their chance, the second mate firing at a whale but unfortunately missing it. The following day two more were seen, but no boat could get near them. There was a very sad occurrence that day, when an Eskimo boat packed with people coming from Haviland Bay, at the head of Repulse Bay, capsized near the ship, drowning eight children and an old woman. Other whales were seen, but on 26th September, when the ice was thick enough for the men to walk from one ship to the other and whaling was finished for that year, none had been killed.

Captain Murray had now spent three winters in the Arctic, and with the experience gained from these, particularly the one he had spent as the mate of the *Perseverance*, he introduced several new ideas to try and make things more comfortable for all hands through the long winter. On the poop a wooden house was built, with its roof covered with turf and topped with blocks of snow, and glass windows were fitted to give as much light as possible. In the house on deck, a large cooking stove was placed for cooking the Eskimo's food and a snow hut was built up against the door of this house, sealing it off and keeping it warm enough for the men to sew boat sails in there. Another snow hut was built over the tiny galley and the doors unshipped, giving the cook plenty of light and fresh air. A big snow hut was also built over the scuttle leading down on to the focsle, with ice windows in its sides, and with the scuttle removed this gave the men much lighter and healthier quarters.

On the 7th October, the ice was cut out to form a dock for the ship's winter berth and it was not long before she was frozen in. With the approach of winter, Captain Murray sent off his Eskimos deer hunting and they arrived back loaded up with venison. A great many deer could be seen on the mainland and Captain Murray records that he sat at the masthead for hours "watching herd after herd of them dancing along the beach migrating to the south round the head of Repulse Bay". One of the young Eskimo harpooners shot forty-five deer in one day and arrived back aboard complaining of feeling very tired, as well he might, for he had spent most of the day skinning the deer he had killed. The ship's crew was variously employed, one of their jobs being to cut freshwater ice from a pond and stack it up near the ship for use through the winter.

Once the winter had set in, the ship's crew worked until noon and had the remainder of the day to themselves. Captain Murray insisted on them taking exercise during their off-time, the rule being that if they would not do so, they must work. Having plenty of deer meat, a deer ham was issued to each member of the crew and hung in the 'tweendecks, to be replenished when necessary. Later in the winter, the Eskimos who were encamped by the ship ran short of food and were given supplies of meat. Captain Murray never gave them flour or any soft, sloppy foods as he considered it spoilt their teeth, but they were given plenty of hard biscuit and as much as possible their own types of food.

Christmas and New Year passed much as they had done in other years and on 7th January (1897) Captain Murray, with his carpenter and six Eskimos and two sledges set off to visit the wreck of the *Desdemona* to see if any stores could be salvaged from her, telling those aboard they would be back in about five days.

Captain Murray gives us an account of this trip, which gives a good idea of what Arctic travel was like in those days:

"I left the ship on a journey down the 'Welcome' to the *Desdemona* and about 4 p.m., we built our snow hut at Beach Point, got into our sleeping bags, and spent a very cold night, for the temperature was forty below zero. To make our coffee in the morning, we had to melt down snow, but the paraffin in our lamps was frozen to the consistency of condensed milk so we had to place them close to an Eskimo stone lamp and thaw the paraffin before we could get the wicks to light. It usually took us about two hours before we could get our drink of coffee. When we arrived at the place where the *Desdemona* had been wrecked, there was nothing to be seen and we assumed that the pack ice must have carried the wreck off the reef. The next morning we built a snow hut and three of the Eskimos went off deer hunting while the other three left to get some salmon meat they had cached further down the 'Welcome'. Three dogs were left with us as a protection against bears as they would give us plenty of warning to get our rifles ready; but as it turned out, these dogs were more of a nuisance than anything else, as they would persist in sleeping on top of the igloo and the heat of their bodies melted the snow, causing it to cave in, so that lying in our sleeping bags we could touch the roof with our hands. The carpenter and I could build up the sides of the igloo all right, but the art of putting on the roof was beyond us. The three Eskimos who had gone off deer hunting arrived back having found none, so after repairing the igloo roof they went off to help the others with their walrus meat.

"On 14th January, 1897, our paraffin oil was finished, and when a search round where the *Desdemona* had been had produced none, we had to do all our cooking over the flame of an Eskimo lamp. It took so long to boil coffee on the lamp that when we wanted something to eat we didn't attempt to cook it but split open a tin of meat, hacked it into pieces with a hatchet and thawed it a bit over the flames. That and hard biscuit was all we had to subsist on.

"On January 16th, the carpenter and I and two Eskimos set off back to the ship with one sledge, the wind being against us and the thermometer at fifty below zero. The carpenter, poor fellow, had to sit with his back to the wind, with his hood around him, because if he faced the wind his nose seemed to freeze up immediately. Sometimes he had to get off his sledge and run to keep his feet warm. We reached one of the igloos we had built on the journey down and after feeding the dogs, had a cold supper and turned into our sleeping bags. The following day we had to face a fresh breeze with the thermometer at forty-five below zero. It was most unusual to have a strong wind with a low thermometer but we got it all right and that was about the only time I wore anything around my neck, borrowing a cravat from an Eskimo and tying it round my neck to prevent the snow getting in.

"Our two natives did not want to travel as they were afraid we would lose ourselves, the loose snow blowing on the surface of the ice made it difficult to see our leaders sometimes, although overhead there was a clear blue sky. That second night we camped in another igloo we had built, at

Beach Point, and the following day reached the ship to find them preparing to send out a search party. Instead of the five days that I had said we would be away, we had been away twelve''.

There appears to have been a suicidal strain among the Eskimos which was not confined to the old, for on the day of Captain Murray's return from this hard trip a young Eskimo who had been ill for a few days hung himself. Strange to say when the *Perseverance* had wintered previously at Repulse Bay this man's father had committed suicide by the same means. Later in the year an old man also did away with himself. There is a macabre air of grim inevitability in the way these old people ended their lives with the full knowledge if not the active assistance of their children. This old man called together his family and explained to them what had to be done; and then took a Martini-Henry rifle which fired an explosive bullet, squatted on the floor, placed the butt of the rifle on the ground and the muzzle under his chin and pressed the trigger, his family being present when he did it. Two days after this, a Nichilik Eskimo arrived on his sledge and said his brother had committed suicide a few days earlier but gave no reason for the act.

The two captains, Mackenzie of the *Platina* and Murray of the *Perseverance*, saw a good deal of each other that winter and although as Captain Murray remarked, they had their points of difference, they remained good friends. All the same, things were run very differently aboard the *Platina* to what they were aboard the Scottish ship. Captain Murray tells us that ''one day during the winter, I noticed two of the sailors belonging to the American ship pulling a small sled with snow, dragging it a distance over the ice, emptying it out, then coming back for another load. They did this for some time and then suddenly reversed the procedure and brought the snow back near the ship again. I asked the captain why they were doing this and he told me that the two men had stolen some mucktuk (whale skin) and were being punished for it. It seemed a funny kind of punishment to me, just crazy''.

Like most of the American whalers the *Platina* had Portuguese (Cape Verde Islanders) among her crew and one day during the winter two of them, boat-steerers, went for a walk on the mainland. Coming back, one of them became exhausted and could go no further, so the other left him and went back aboard for help. Search parties were sent out that night but could not find him and had to return and it was assumed that the man must have died. The next day, the cook of the *Perseverance*, up in the crow's nest looking round, spotted a figure on the ice and a sledge party was immediately sent out. They found the missing man staggering about in a dazed condition but such is the resilience of the human body that within a day or two he had quite recovered from his experience.

The *Platina*, like all the other American whalers which found their way up into the Arctic in Captain Murray's day, was a very old ship, having been built at Rochester, Mass., USA in 1847.

Besides those Eskimos actually employed by the ship, a number of others lived by her and used her as an entertainment hall of a night, playing draughts and dominoes. The mothers used to bring their children and leave them to play about on the floor of the deckhouse where it was warm. The physical state of the children was a good indication of the skill of the father as a hunter; if a child had a pot belly one could be fairly certain that its father was a poor hunter, who gave his children an excess of food at one time and not enough at another. Captain Murray said that he always found that the children with normal stomachs had fathers who were good hunters. One child in particular he tells us about:

"I had noticed for some time a small boy of four or five who would sit in a corner and never play with the other children and who was poorly clothed and apparently half-starved. I made enquiries and found he had been adopted by an old woman who was treating him very badly and sometimes even made him sleep in the outer igloo with the husky dogs. Such treatment as this was very rare, for the Eskimos were all very good to their children. One day the child had a black eye, so I called the old woman on deck and told her it was very wrong to adopt a child at all, when she herself had to rely on charity. I said I would give her a cooking pan, a few yards of print, some tobacco and other items, in exchange for the boy, and she agreed to this offer. I then gave the boy to a young couple, knowing that the husband was a good hunter. Within a few days the child was wearing new clothes and was soon as lively and healthy-looking as any of the other children. But the story did not have a happy ending. The young couple told me that they were quite sure that as soon as I left, the old woman would come round whining to have the child back again, and as she was an angout (medicine woman or priest) they could do nothing but give him back. This is exactly what happened and when I returned later she went away inland with the child and kept out of my sight all the time I was there".

Unusual though it was for Eskimos to ill-treat their children, Captain Murray gave it as his opinion,that one reason for the decline in population of the Eskimos, was the habit of the parents giving their children to other couples, who did not always treat them properly.

On 22nd April, 1897, all the ship's Eskimos and some of the boats were sent down to Beach Point, at the southern entrance to Repulse Bay, and on May 17th, the ship's crew was sent down to join them. A few days later the pack ice had cleared away sufficiently for Captain Murray to cruise down Roe's Welcome to see what conditions were like at Whale Point, as he intended stationing three boats at Whale Point again. Finding conditions bad, he returned and cruised in the boats over towards Frozen Straits, just North of Southampton Island.

The Eskimos were very careless with firearms and many accidents resulted from this. One such occurred while the boats were lying at the floe edge near Frozen Straits on the lookout for whales. One of the Eskimos in another boat was playing about with his rifle when it went off, the bullet passing between two of the men in Captain Murray's boat. Fortunately for him he was sitting in the sternsheets. He says: "I jumped out of the boat and round to the other one to find out how the accident happened and gave the man a blessing in the best Eskimo language I could muster". Captain Murray said that time after time he had warned the Eskimos about being careless with firearms, but all his warnings did not prevent another accident later, with a less fortunate ending. Some of the boats were in the vicinity of Beach Point, shooting white whales, when one of the Eskimos laid down his rifle, fully loaded and cocked. Something fouling the trigger, the rifle went off and sent a bullet through the knee joint of one man and through the hip of another. About this accident Captain Murray remarked:

"I was mighty glad it did not happen to any of my white crew as there were three of them, in the boat at that time. We had to leave the bullet in the second man's hip as I did not feel I was enough of a surgeon to take it out. The first man, the one with the shattered knee joint, was left by the natives at Beach Point. I sent the boat back immediately to bring him to the ship but when they got to the place the next day, they found him lying dead where they had left him the previous day, just above high water mark. I suppose he just bled to death, as there was no-one there to help him".

There was always a good deal of rivalry among the whale ships where the capture of whales was concerned and during the time the *Perseverance* and the *Platina* were in company there were two examples of this, although some people might use a stronger word than 'rivalry' for the conduct of some of the *Platina*'s people. On first arriving at Repulse Bay, the captain of the *Platina* had suggested that if either of them had raised a whale, the other would keep clear, and this was readily agreed to by Captain Murray. One day he was up in the crow's nest when he saw some of his boats, manned by Eskimos, which had been lying at the floe edge, suddenly put out as though in pursuit of a whale, although he could see no sign of one. Soon the boats of the *Platina* also headed out to sea in the same direction as the *Perseverance*'s boats. When the Eskimos returned aboard that evening Captain Murray asked if they had seen a whale and it was then explained to him that no whales had been seen but the Eskimos wanted to find out if the *Platina* intended to keep to the agreement and had used this method to do so! Captain Murray remarked that he thought it "pretty slick" of his Eskimos to have thought up this means of testing their rivals. "I went aboard the *Platina* and had a talk with the captain and told him a few home truths and said I wanted fair whaling. If he wasn't going to stick to his agreement then it was all right with me, because I had ten boats to his five and he'd come off worst. If he started the foul play I'd finish it".

During the winter Captain Murray had been reading a book of Arctic voyages by Parry in which the author stated that a number of whales had been seen in Duke of York Bay, on the north coast of Southampton Island, and in an unguarded moment he had mentioned to the captain of the *Platina* that he intended going there the following summer to look for whales. On the 8th August he set off with this intention and meeting three of his boats, cruising for whales near the mouth of Frozen Straits was informed that the mate of the *Platina* had passed that way heading for Duke of York Bay. Taking the stores from his three boats he sent them back to the ship for more for themselves and pressed on through Frozen Straits into Duke of York Bay. There was no signs of the *Platina*'s boats and they only showed up after he had been cruising in the Bay for three days.

"I sailed over to them but they did not seem to want any conversation", Captain Murray recorded. "They had tried to slip away quietly from Repulse Bay and were very annoyed to see I had got there before them". As it turned out, not a single whale was seen by either party in Duke of York Bay and both returned to their ships after a futile trip. Regarding Duke of York Bay, it was discovered by Sir John Parry in 1821 and described by him as "one of the most extensive and secure harbours in the world".

Captain Murray was certainly not a man to take offence quickly but his ire was aroused by some of the crew of his winter neighbour, the *Platina*, and he has recorded the following: "Although there were a few things the other captain and I didn't see eye to eye about we managed to remain very good friends. But before my arrival, one of his Portuguese boat-steerers had caught a whale and since then he had made a god of the man. It was 'Pedro this' and 'Pedro that' until one day I told the captain: 'In some of the states in America you'd be ashamed to be seen on the same sidewalk with him'. I suppose I was a bit prejudiced about his Portuguese boat-steerers, as I had heard two of them passing remarks about the 'dirty Scotsmen'. I didn't know whether the remark was made about the ship or the men, but anyway it got my back up. Our ship certainly was dirty compared with the Americans as we were using soft coal in the galley all the time, which dirtied the snow round the ship, while the Americans used hard coal, which gave off very little smoke. I told the captain what I had heard and said: "Our ship may be dirty but our men, no". I told him that any one of my sailors probably had more clothes in his chest than half of his crew possessed. I suggested that I should call two of my men aboard his ship and he could bring along two of his men, without telling them what was being done, and we'd have them strip off their top clothes. I was willing to place a heavy bet that my men would have cleaner underclothes than his men. The other captain shook his head. "I'm not taking it on. Dammit, cap, it's only the other day I threatened to take two of my men aft and sand and canvas them if they didn't try to keep themselves a bit cleaner!" My own opinion was that living down in the focsle, where they had nothing but seal oil lamps, his men didn't have a chance to keep clean; the American sailors seemed to be nice fellows and I felt sorry for them having to live in conditions like those".

Quite a number of whales were seen that summer in the near Repulse Bay but they were all very shy and restless and difficult to approach, probably due partly to the shallow water. On August 21st, the *Perseverance* got her first whale of the season, an Eskimo harpooner Angaatingmaring killing it. On September 5th, the *Platina* killed a small whale and two days later Captain Murray himself killed a big one. All the *Perseverance*'s boats except his own being away on the lookout for whales and the day being fine, he decided to take his boat out for a cruise and had with him an Eskimo man and four boys—what was called a 'scrap' crew. He describes the incident as follows: "We ran out clear of the islands when we spotted two whales blowing away out to the eastward. Being a fresh westerly breeze, I ran down towards them but as the whales appeared to be coming to the west, I hauled the boat to and lay with a slack sheet. At their next rising the two whales came up about 200 feet ahead of my boat, so we pulled in the sheet and sailed right in between the two. We struck the larger one, which rose right under the boat and lifted it right up. The boat slipped off the whale's back and the gunwale went right under the water and half-filled the boat. Then the whale on the other side raised itself up to make the plunge and struck the boat on its port side and almost turned it over. By this time the Eskimo boys were clinging to the thwart and shouting with fear. We were well fast, the whale having got an explosive bomb lance along with the harpoon and at the next rising we hauled up alongside it and I gave it five bomb lances from the shoulder gun. It started to blow blood and was almost dead before the other boats came to our assistance. But before she turned flukes-up she had smashed a few oars of the other boats and nearly upset one of them. We then started towing the whale back to the harbour and pulled it up at high water, let the tide go back and started to flence it. It proved to be a good whale, the bone measuring ten feet six inches long. The same day the *Platina* killed a baby whale with bone six inches long".

It was this sort of action which was partly responsible for the growing scarcity of whales.

After that, the weather became very unsettled and with strong winds preventing the boats from going out to look for whales, no more were caught that season. With winter not far away, the two barques made preparations to leave for home and on 13th September the *Platina* hove up and sailed. She struck on a reef for a time but got clear and sailed away. The *Perseverance* sailed the following day and after calling at Whale Point to land the Eskimos set out for Peterhead. One gets some idea of Arctic navigation in Captain Murray's day from the experiences of the *Perseverance* that year. From leaving Repulse Bay on the 14th September until the 28th, the sun was seen only once, the barque working on dead reckoning the whole way until she got into Hudson Strait. On 2nd October, Resolution Island, at the entrance to Hudson Strait, was passed and the anchors were then taken aboard and the chain stowed below. The vessel was leaking very badly at this time, due to the rough treatment she had received in the ice, the water being over the keelson, and on October 6th both pumps became choked. Two of the crew, floundering about in the icy water in between the blubber tanks, eventually succeeded in clearing them and probably saved the barque from foundering. From then until 19th October, they met continual bad weather, with the decks constantly awash, and arrived at Peterhead on 27th October, 1897 "after a hard voyage with little success", to quote Captain Murray.

The termination of this voyage saw the end of Captain Murray's long association with the *Perseverance*. He had served in her as Ordinary Seaman, A.B., second mate, mate and master and spent four winters in the Arctic aboard her. It would seem that the Hudson's Bay Company was not satisfied with the results of their trial at the whaling, for the *Perseverance* was next sold to an Aberdeen firm who employed her fishing for salmon in Cumberland Gulf. But she did not last much longer, being posted missing in the autumn of 1901 when homeward-bound from the Arctic. She was 49 years old at the time of her loss.

After spending the winter of 1897/98 at home, Captain Murray sailed as mate of the steam whaling barque *Active*, with his brother Alex in command, on a whaling voyage to Hudson Straits and Hudson Bay. The *Active* was a vessel of 348 gross tons built at Peterhead in 1852 as a sailing whaler, ship-rigged, and had as her first commander, Captain David Gray, who was later to become known as "the Prince of Whalers" because of his success at the "fishing". It is an indication of the profitable nature of whaling in the 1860's that in 1866 the *Active* was sold and Captain Gray had a ship built for himself by Alexander Hall of Aberdeen. This was the *Eclipse*, described by Basil Lubbock as "perhaps the most famous of all the latter-day Scottish whalers". In 1871 the *Active* had engines installed and about the same time changed her port of registry from Peterhead to Dundee. In 1875 her rig was altered from ship to barque and she continued whaling under the various owners. When Captain Murray joined her in 1898 she was owned by R. Kinnes of Dundee and was 46 years old. In those years she had many a nip in the ice, the most serious being in 1877, when she was so badly squeezed, her hatches were diamond-shaped.

By 1898 whales had become so scarce that ships were killing anything that would produce a profit and this voyage the *Active* was looking for walrusses. There is a fair amount of blubber on a walrus and at that time the oil brought about £18 a ton. The hide, used for bicycle seats among other things, brought about 1/6 a pound and walrus ivory was valued at 2/6 a pound. Walrusses are very difficult to catch, for if shot and killed they will sink immediately and the only satisfactory method of securing them was by harpoon. Admiral Sir Leopold McLintock in his book "The Voyage of the *Fox* in Arctic Seas" says: "A walrus was shot through the head by a Minie bullet, none other will penetrate such a massive skull. Unfortunately for my collection of specimens, and for the dogs, the animal sank". They can be savage at times and are a formidable foe when roused. One day that season in the *Active*, John was out after walrusses and was wearing a red shirt. This apparently had the same effect upon the walrusses as it would have upon a bull and several of them attacked the boat, making holes in it with their tusks so that it was in danger of sinking. There would have been little hope for the boat's crew if this had happened, but they managed to get back to the ship, where the boat was hove up, the holes patched with sheets of lead and they set off again to resume hunting. Such incidents were taken as being all in the day's work in the whalers.

No whales were caught this season and the *Active* returned to Dundee with 150 walrusses and 17 polar bears which certainly could not have given any profits for the voyage. She put into Aberdeen, windbound, on her homeward voyage and while there, two reporters boarded her to obtain news of the voyage. The captain, being very tired, told them he would see them the next day and sent them along to the steward. The latter was very drunk, and apparently not caring overmuch for reporters, chased them round the deck with a poker before they were put ashore in a boat. In all the upset the steward smashed his only bottle of whisky and sat there with tears rolling down his cheeks. The so-called "convict ship" *Success* was on exhibition in Dundee at the same time and John Murray told his friends: "Why bother to go and see her—we've plenty of convicts aboard here!"

CHAPTER SEVEN

SOUTHAMPTON ISLAND

ALTHOUGH no whales had been killed that voyage, two or three were sighted near Southampton Island, in the northern part of Hudson's Bay and an American whaling schooner reported having seen several and killed a few in the same vicinity. As a result of these reports the owners of the *Active*, Messrs, R. Kinnes, decided to set up a whaling and trading station on Southampton Island and put Captain John Murray in charge of it. Accordingly, the *Active* left Dundee on 1st May, 1899, with Captain Alex Murray in command and his brother aboard with the timber and stores for the projected post. The venture did not start too well, as John Murray tells us: "On 22nd May, we reached in on the pack ice a long distance east of Resolution Island and ran up north along the edge of the pack to near Franklin Island, where we started working our way into the pack, making poor progress. We lay for days beset, unable to move, the ship being carried south by the south-west current. Every effort was made to work to the eastward to reach the clear water, but when nearing the edge of the pack ice, we encountered a heavy swell and with the vessel being badly banged about, we were afraid of losing our propeller. After reaching the clear water, we worked north again and then entered the ice and worked to the westward, through the pack, reaching the land on the north side of Frobisher Bay (Frobisher Bay is a large inlet to the north of Hudson Strait, which leads into Hudson Bay). "We sighted a large number of walrusses and killed about thirty and then cruised about under sail waiting an opportunity of getting to the eastward. Our second mate injured his leg through a walrus rolling on top of him, but as the bone was not broken, he got well in a few days. On 28th June, three boats went on shore at a small island and loaded themselves up with eider duck eggs. Next day, one boat went to the island and brought back a lot more eggs. We salted them down in all the boxes and barrels we could find, some of the crew even using their sea chests for this purpose. Meanwhile, we cruised about in Frobisher Bay picking up a few walrusses every day and on 8th July started working through the ice to the eastward. At midnight on the 10th July, we were close to Cape Best, Resolution Island, the whaler *Polar Star* of Dundee in company. She having lost the blades of her propeller, we took her in tow into Ashe Inlet, where we were met by the Eskimos who had sailed in the ship the previous year. We took them on board, men, women and children, and after cleaning out the 'tweendecks put them in there, sails being hung from the deckhead as curtains and stopped-up during the day. The men were supplied with a suit of clothes and underwear when they joined the ship and the ladies given print cloth to make dresses for themselves. While on board, the Eskimo men were allowed a pound of tobacco a month, the women half a pound".

On 28th July, the *Active* arrived at Cape Low, southernmost tip of Southampton Island, and started to look for a suitable place to establish a trading post. A spot handy to a fresh water pond was decided on as a site for the post and on 31st July they started landing timber and stores. "We saw one Southampton Island Eskimo and his two wives and children", Captain Murray said. "They were all completely covered with grease from the carcase of a whale lying on the beach which they were cutting up. It had been killed by the American sailing schooner *Era* which reported having killed seven whales that spring off Southampton Island". The site for the base was north-east of Cape Low, at a place now marked on the chart as Hut Point.

On 2nd August, all stores having been landed, the *Active* left to resume her whaling and walrussing, leaving Captain Murray in charge of the post. With him he had a carpenter and a cook, both of them from Peterhead and like himself, unmarried. The purpose of having a carpenter with him, was primarily to repair the whaleboats which were frequently damaged by ice or walrusses. As regards the cook, the first thing Captain Murray impressed upon him was that he must be clean, to set the natives a good example. Until they had built their house they lived in a tent made out of an old mainsail borrowed from the *Active*, which returned on 11th August bringing a number of Eskimos from Roes Welcome. She left again on 14th August and that was the last, the three white men were to see of her until the following year. Captain Murray was not to know it until the next year but after leaving him the *Active* and the *Polar Star* encountered vey bad weather and much ice, with the result that in October the *Polar Star* had to be abandoned, her crew and what Arctic produce she had being taken aboard the *Active*. The *Polar Star* was a barque built at Peterhead in 1857, slightly smaller than the *Active* and at the time of her loss owned, like her, by R. Kinnes of Dundee. These two ships had formed part of the fleet of four whalers which in September 1892 had left Dundee for the Antarctic in search of the Southern Right whale, the others being the *Balaena* and the *Diana*. The voyage was a complete failure and the vessels returned without having even seen a solitary right whale.

At the time of Captain Murray's sojourn on Southampton Island it was still largely unexplored, even though it had been visited by Sir Thomas Button as far back as 1612, nearly 300 years earlier—an indication of how the Arctic had been left alone until comparatively recently. Captain Murray had now created quite a little township on the island, the first it had ever known. He had about sixty Eskimo men working for him, and with them their wives and children, These men belonged to the Ivilik, Nichilik and Kinapartoo tribes, none of them being natives of Southampton Island. The Iviliks, who came from Repulse Bay and Roe's Welcome, were good deer hunters; the Nichiliks, who were from King William Land, near the Magnetic Pole, were the best sealers. The Kinapartoos came from Chesterfield Inlet. There were six whaleboats and as winter approached it was the practise to allow two of them to go off deer hunting while the other four cruised in search of whales.

The deer hunting served the double purpose of providing food and also winter clothing for the natives. Only two whales had been seen since arrival and none had been killed when the formation of the ice, on the water, put a stop to any further whaling for that year. At that time, the island was alive with bears. One had greeted them when they first arrived and Captain Murray related how, on one occasion, he and his brother shot eleven bears in one afternoon. In the summertime a bear's coat was in poor condition and of little value and he had to stop the Eskimos shooting them as he wanted them to kill whales, not bears. The flesh of a young bear made good eating but the Europeans did not use it much, leaving it mostly for the Eskimos. Young walrus meat Captain Murray regarded as very good eating. He was a very keen hunter and in September and October of that year shot enough ptarmigan to last the whole winter.

On 23rd September, an Eskimo called Kyaa died after a long illness and soon afterwards two young babies died. Captain Murray had plenty to say about infant mortality among the Eskimos:

"Most of the deaths are among those babies who have been adopted at a very early age, generally just a few weeks old. They cannot be breast-fed so the foster mother chews meat and then squirts the juice into the baby's mouth. They seem to think this will be adequate and are very surprised when the baby simply fades away and dies of starvation". Just before Christmas, the wife of an Eskimo called Taomung gave birth to a male child which when only a week or so old, was given to a young woman who had no child of her own. Within a month the baby had died from the usual cause, starvation.

Once the whaling had been stopped by the ice, the Eskimos were employed in deer and bear-hunting and on 21st November, a party arrived back from a trip to the northern part of the island and reported having seen a large number of wolves feeding on the carcase of a whale which had been cast up on the beach. As they had been told that the Southampton Island wolves were very ferocious, even attacking the husky dogs by the huts, they had left them undisturbed. To ensure a supply of fresh water well into the winter, a hole was cut in the ice over a pond at the settlement and an igloo built over it. Another igloo was then built on, covering the door of the one over the hole to prevent it getting snowed up, and in the second igloo the blacksmith's forge was placed. The heat from this, soon melted the snow on the inside of the igloo, the forge was removed and when the melted snow had become ice, it made an excellant place for storing water.

Christmas and the New Year passed, much as they had done in Captain Murray's earlier winters in the Arctic, with the Eskimos all attending a big feast and dance on New Year's Day. There were frequent visits from bears and one night one actually entered the outer igloo, where the dogs were kept, of an Eskimo dwelling. It was chased out by the dogs and shot by an Eskimo. On another occasion Captain Murray was aroused by the barking of the dogs and grabbing his rifle ran out to find the cause of the commotion. He found a bear surrounded by huskies but could not get a shot at it because it kept its head down, looking at the dogs. When it finally raised its head Captain Murray fired at it but in the tangle of bear and dogs unfortunately shot one of the latter. Regarding Eskimo dogs, he told me that he was only once bitten by one, quite unexpectantly. Getting an Eskimo woman to tie up the animal, he gave it a good thrashing as the most certain method of teaching it to behave.

1900 is a long time ago but even then there were not so many places left unexplored and their inhabitants untouched by so-called civilisation. On Southampton Island, Captain Murray had the experience of contacting natives, some of whom had never seen a white man. He gives the following account of his meeting with them:

"On April 1st (1900) about 6 p.m., six sledges came in sight which we made out to be Southampton Island Eskimos (Sidlermuits). There were eight men with their families and they all stood on a raised piece of ground half a mile from the house looking at us. I told my Eskimos to go over and invite them to come down to the house, but they were reluctant to do so and when I asked the reason they told me they would like to fight the Sidlermuits for coming down to their land". (This seems a little unfair, for it was really Captain Murray's Eskimos who were the intruders!) I told them: 'No , they want to be friendly', so they agreed to go and bring them down if I allowed them to take their rifles with them. I could not allow that so I went off by myself, round the end of the lake, and going up to the strangers, shook hands with all of them. To let them know I was friendly I had to wear a smile on my face the whole time. They crowded round me, stretching out their hands to feel the cloth jacket I was wearing in the warm weather. My Eskimos, seeing the strangers were friendly, next came running towards us at full speed and I told them to tell the Sidlermuits I wanted them to come down to the house. On the way, the Sidlermuits were hanging on to me to such an extent I could hardly manage to walk, some of them jumping backwards and forwards like dogs round a horse and all of them shouting and their dogs barking. It appeared that only two or three of these people had ever seen a white man before. When we got to the house the cook served out coffee and ship's biscuit to our men and also to the Sidlermuits. At first they spat out the biscuit but it did not take them long, to get to like it, as much as my own Eskimos. I took two of the newcomers to my room with one of the Iviliks as an interpreter, as I found that the Sidlermuits' dialect was somewhat different. I tried to teach them to pronounce all the letters of the English dialect and found that they quickly learned to do so, much better than the other Eskimos, most of whom cannot pronounce "f" and "s". The Sidlermuits had rather soft, melodious voices.

"I was trying to find out if they had seen any whales near South Bay, where they lived, when I noticed one of the men I had in my room acting in a strange way. He was crouching in a corner, smiling and nodding up at a calendar hanging on the wall which had a picture of a woman on it. Then he ran crouching along the wall, never taking his eyes off the picture. I asked the other man if he was crazy, but he said that he wasn't and asked him why he was behaving like that. It appeared that the woman in the picture, kept her eyes on him wherever he went and he couldn't stop looking at her! Outside, I found my Eskimos talking to the newcomers. Already they had taught them what to say to me and every time I passed one man he would keep on saying 'Hullo, what now?' I asked the Sidlermuits why they had not paid us a visit before this and was amazed to hear that they could not build a snow hut and as a result were unable to travel during the winter. They were the only Eskimos I had heard of, who could not build an igloo. The coastal parts of Southampton Island are largely composed of limestone, often in flat pieces, and the Sidlermuits used these for the walls of their houses, filling up the crevices with moss and roofing them, with the skins of animals. They were all in a filthy condition, their clothes impregnated with oily soot from the lamps they used. The other tribes would beat out the flames which were round the edges of their lamps and get a clean small flame, but the Southampton Island natives did not seem to know how to do this and their lamps used to give off clouds of smoke and soot. This was undoubtedly the reason why they all seemed to have lung trouble, from which many of them died.

"The day after the Sidlermuits arrived I took them together with my own Eskimos outside the house, put a tin, on a rock, some little distance away and got my men to fire at it. This seemed to delight the newcomers. Then I picked out the most intelligent looking one of them, and told one of my own Eskimos, to show him how to hold and aim a rifle. He would not hold the butt close to his shoulder, so that when he fired the recoil got him, but this only made him laugh uproariously. He did not hit the target of course. After the lesson, I gave him a muzzle-loading rifle with bullets, cap and powder and the other Eskimos took him in hand to teach him how to use it. I also got the Sidlermuits to show us what they could do with their bows and arrows and must say they made mighty poor shooting with them. The arrow heads were made of flint and the shafts mostly from driftwood. The bows were made of caribou antler seized together with sinew, which was also used for the bow string. These Sidlermuits were smaller in stature than the Iviliks and the Hudson Strait Eskimos and their clothes, made of bearskin, were cut the same as those of the natives of Cape York and Davis Straits, far to the east. A few years after this, in 1905, all the Southampton Island natives died of an internal complaint something like dysentery and when I returned there in that year, there was only one young woman and two children who had been adopted two or three years before by the Iviliks, and the young woman was then very far gone with consumption. She received all the care possible from both the Iviliks and my own men, but she just wasted away and died the following winter. It is a strange fact that, in the same year that all the Sidlermuits died, a large number of Eskimos at Lake Harbour (on the north side of Hudson Strait), Davis Straits and in Labrador also died of the same complaint". In reporting the decimation of the Southampton Island natives the "Arctic Pilot, Vol. 3", calls the sickness "suggestive of typhoid" and says that for some years afterwards the island was uninhabited.

About the time the Sidlermuits showed themselves, the boats were put in the water and commenced cruising on the lookout for whales. The first one was seen on the 4th May and although it was harpooned, the harpoon drew and it got away. It was the sort of incident which made all the difference between success and failure on a venture of this sort, for one whale might represent £3000 of oil and bone. An average whale might produce about twenty tons of oil at approximately £22 a ton and perhaps a ton of bone at £2500 a ton. On 10th June, they had better luck and killed a whale. It was towed into the beach and left there for the Eskimo women to strip off its blubber and bone, while the boats went off, to resume their hunt for whales. On 8th July, three of the boats had an unpleasant experience while out hunting for walruses. Getting in among the walrusses, all three boats were damaged by their quarry and one walruss jumped right out of the water into a boat, nearly capsizing it but fortunately rolling out again as the boat went over. They were lucky, for a walrus can weigh a ton or more. It was customary to carry sheet lead and canvas in the boats for quick repairs and although some of the Eskimos were in the water for a long time no lives were lost and they were able to pull the boats up on the ice and effect temporary repairs.

The system under which the Eskimos worked for Captain Murray was a quite simple and unambiguous one. They were in his direct employ, manning the whaleboats in the summer and hunting on land for him in the winter. At the whaling, each man received six pounds of biscuit a week, a quantity of molasses, coffee, marmalade and butter, and these supplies were taken by dog sledge every week to wherever the boats were stationed. During the time they were whaling, the Eskimos would kill seals, and the meat they did not use was taken back for the use of their wives and children, encamped round the trading post. Eskimos have truly enormous appetites and are also completely improvident, and for this latter reason were never given too many stores at one time, if this were done they would eat the lot before starting the hunting for which they were being employed. They were supplied with rifles and ammunition and in winter, when there was no whaling, would go off hunting, sometimes for months at a time. Apart from the deer, which provided them with food and clothing, all the bear, wolf, fox and seal skins they obtained were the property of their employer. With the trading post the only shop within thousands of miles, money was useless to them and in effect the return for their labours was that they were completely maintained in everything they needed. As a result of having to come into contact with missionaries, some of the Eskimos wanted Sunday as a holiday during the summer months, that all too short period which was the only time when whales could be caught. Captain Murray's answer to this was short and to the point: he told them that they could have seven Sundays a week, during the winter, but in the summer he wanted them seven days a week.

There can have been few men who knew the old-time Eskimo better than Captain Murray and his opinion of them was unqualifiedly good. He regarded them as Nature's children and despite reports to the contrary never found them dishonest. He adapted it as a principle never to make them a promise he could not fulfil and in this way won their respect and trust. Eskimos are possessed of a high degree of intelligence and within a few weeks some of the children had learned to read religious books received by Captain Murray from a missionary. The adults also learned to write in English and during the whaling season, some of the women even sent letters to their husbands down at the floe edge. These letters they would read to the sled driver, taking supplies down to the men and off he would go. Having arrived, he would first read out the contents of any letters he had for the men and then hand them over, so the "postal service" could hardly be called a confidential one!

It was during this stay at Southampton Island that Captain Murray had an experience with a polar bear that might have put a finish to any more whaling for him. One day in the early Spring of 1901, he was walking along the beach on the lookout for a seal or some other food for the dogs when he spotted a polar bear on the young ice which formed every night on the sea between the land and the pack ice. The bear was gliding along with her feet well apart to spread her weight, and an adult bear weighing far more than a man, Captain Murray reasoned that if the ice would support the weight of a bear, it would be quite safe for him to follow it. Accordingly he went on the ice and within about sixty feet of the bear fired at it—and only grazed its shoulder. Saltwater ice is more elastic than the freshwater variety and the recoil of the shot, put just sufficient extra weight on his feet to send him through the ice up to his armpits. He was dressed in sealskin trousers and long boots which were tied below the knees with a piece of sinew and were completely watertight, so that with a strong current running under the ice, his legs were kept well up to the surface under the ice. So there he was, almost completely helpless, unable to raise himself for fear he broke the ice on which his arms were resting. The report of the shot at first startled the bear but then it moved towards him, to investigate what sort of an animal it was, that could make such a noise, and as Captain Murray told me: "I thought I was surely bound for the Happy Hunting Grounds". If he let go of the ice he would be drawn under it and drowned; and if he didn't let go, one swipe of the bear's paw would kill him as easily as one would swat a fly. And yet, with the bear advancing towards him and death apparently not far away, his natural courage and refusal to accept the seemingly inevitable still asserted themselves and when the bear was about ten feet away from him, looking enormous, he suddenly yelled with all the power of his lungs. It was the only possible thing left for him to do, and it worked, for the bear halted and then turned and slowly walked away, apparently either frightened or perhaps not liking the smell of him. When it had gone he was able to raise himself onto the ice and made his way to the settlement.

Captain Murray stayed at Southampton Island for three years and one received the impression that the life there, isolated though it was, suited him. A great hunter, he would often go off on hunting trips of a week or more, leaving the other two to look after the post. Every summer the *Active*, with his brother still in command, would bring him stores and take away the result of the year's hunting and whaling. The blubber taken from captured whales was kept in tanks which had been landed from the *Active* when the post was first established. These tanks, nesting one inside another, had originally been put aboard to be used as "overflow" tanks if the ship were ever lucky enough to fill her permanent tanks. In latter days, at least, the tanks had never been needed. Captain Murray always left one of them open for the use of the Eskimos, for food and fuel.

One rather strange incident during his stay on Southampton Island concerned twins, both boys, born to an Eskimo woman. It is very rare for twins to be born to Eskimos, although Captain Murray had heard of one case of triplets. For some reason known only to herself the mother of the twins, a widow with one older child, took the line that the twins had been conceived without a father and never did disclose his name. Petual, an Eskimo who had imbibed some vague ideas about Christianity through constant contact with the Lake Harbour natives and called himself a "Jesusy man" saw in this an analogy with the Immaculate Conception of our Lord and professed to believe the woman. Hearing that she was contemplating infanticide Captain Murray took some Eskimos with him and visited the woman to tell her he would not allow this. Instead, he proposed that the twins should be adopted by others, a plan to which she readily agreed. Petual was that rather dangerous character, a religious fanatic, and spread abroad a fantastic story about a journey he had just made up to Heaven. On arrival at the Pearly Gates he had been stopped (one supposes by St. Peter) and was told that he would have to die first before he could enter. But the celestial one informed him that as some compensation for his long and unrewarded journey up from Earth, he would be allowed to rename all his tribe when he got back, and a list of names was given for this purpose. As soon as Petual got back to Earth the renaming commenced and Captain Murray recorded that he "found difficulty in remembering all the new names and they were a little hurt when I called them by their old ones". Petual's journey to Heaven had one result which may have been good, for he found on the trip that his long hair impeded his progress and when he got back ordered all the members of the tribe, men and women, to cut their hair short. Captain Murray remarked that "I must say I did not approve of the looks of the older ladies".

During this stay at Southampton Island there was an example of the Eskimos' remarkable ability to withstand cold and hardship. One of them went out seal-hunting and was sitting on the edge of the ice waiting for a seal to come up and give him the chance of a shot at it. The wind was off the land and it was snowing. Suddenly the man realised he was adrift on his floe, being blown along by the wind until he brought up against the pack ice far out at sea. Fortunately for him there was a number of walrusses on the pack ice and he was able to kill two, which gave him food. He was adrift for a week before the wind changed and blew the ice back on the land again and he was able to walk back to the post. When he arrived his foot-gear was completely worn out and he had had no food for two days. He went to sleep immediately he arrived and when he woke up seemed none the worse for an experience which would have killed most white men.

As has been shown, the good days of whaling in the Arctic were now finished and Captain Murray's employers, Messrs. Robert Kinnes, whose address, East Whale Lane, Dundee, gives a good idea of their activities, were finding it necessary to turn to other fields to supplement the dwindling profits from whaling. During the three years spent at Southampton Island, the *Active* brought men out from Peterhead to work at deposits of mica and graphite found at Lake Harbour, in the part known as Meta Incognita, on the north side of Hudson Strait. The men could only work in the summer months and the scheme was not a success and was later abandoned.

In August 1902, just three years after he went there, Captain

Murray was relieved by a man called Brown and went home to Peterhead in the *Active* for a holiday. During his stay at Southampton Island, he kept a record of births and deaths among the Eskimos and the picture the statistics give, is not a happy one. From September 23rd, 1899 to February 1st, 1902 there were twelve births; six young children aged between a few days and two months died, together with ten adults, the majority of whom were very old men and women. In that small community of about sixty families, therefore, the death rate exceeded the birth rate and the population was a dwindling one.

In the Spring of 1903, Captain Murray went out again in the *Active* to take over the post he had started on Southampton Island. When they arrived they could see a ketch at anchor and this proved to be the *Ernest William*, brought out by Messrs. Kinnes to supplement the whaleboats at the "fishing". The *Ernest William* had been built as a North Sea fisherman and was one of several such craft taken out to Hudson's Bay to assist at the whaling. Others were the *Problem*, the *Forget-Me-Not* and the *Queen Bess*. The experiment was a courageous one but not particularly lucky. The *Problem* foundered in the North Atlantic on her way out, her crew being rescued; the *Forget-Me-Not*, after being frozen-in at Frobisher Bay was later rescued by Peary in Captain Murray's old ship the *Windward*, and the *Queen Bess* was for some time used as a depot ship for the mica miners at Lake Harbour.

The *Ernest William* had wintered in South Bay, Southampton Island, and at the break-up of the ice in the Spring had been blown out to sea with only one man and an old Eskimo woman and a child aboard. Unable to hoist the big mainsail by himself, the sailor had managed to set enough canvas to enable him to sail the ketch to the settlement established by Captain Murray. This was a little drama which would certainly find mention in the newspapers today but was thought little of at that time. When the *Active* arrived, Eskimos boarded with a story that three whaleboats had been lost but this was later found to be an exaggeration, only one boat having been lost. The Eskimos, without whom nothing could be achieved, seemed to be getting tired of the Southampton Island project and as a result, the plan of operations was radically altered. Captain Murray took over the *Ernest William*, all the Eskimos who had been working for Kinnes were taken aboard the *Active* and she then towed the ketch right up Roe's Welcome to Repulse Bay, where Captain Murray had decided he would winter. One real difficulty he had to get round was that when he joined the *Ernest William* he found she had only one anchor, and it with only one fluke, three anchors having been lost in gales the previous Fall. So he devised an anchor of sorts, by building round the shank of the anchor, a box which was filled with stones and lashed with chain. Having arrived at Repulse Bay, they set about whaling, but none was caught before the winter set in.

During the winter of 1903/04 Captain Murray received a note from an American called Cleveland who was at a point further down Roe's Welcome, near where the *Desdemona* had been wrecked in 1896. He had been left there by the American whaling schooner *Francis Allyn* years before to trade with the Eskimos and when he sent the note asking for a few small articles such as a sheath knife and one or two other items, had been in the Arctic about seven years. He was completely out of stores and was living as a native. The *Francis Allyn*, a tiny vessel of only 111 tons gross, built at Duxbury, Mass. in 1869, was owned in New Bedford by Thomas Luce, who at this time had a fleet of five whaling schooners, one of them the well-known *Era*. Captain Murray knew of the conditions under which Cleveland was living, and feeling that no white man should go so completely native when help was available, replied in characteristic fashion that he would send him nothing; but if Cleveland cared to come and see him he would offer him hospitality. Accordingly, the American visited him and as it transpired, entered his employ. He had a few furs, the sole result of his hard and solitary existence among the Esquimaux, and wanted Captain Murray to take them. This he declined to do, fortunately as it turned out. The following Spring, the *Era* appeared, with Captain George Comer in commmand. This vessel being owned by Luce Captain Comer, mindful of his owner's interests, demanded from Cleveland all the equipment and Arctic produce he imagined him to be holding. Of equipment there was absolutely none and the few furs Cleveland had he refused to hand over, so Captain Comer proposed that they should fight for possession of them. Cleveland being quite agreeable to this, the two men fought, with unfortunate results for Captain Comer. There is something about this incident particularly fitting to the grim surroundings in which it took place and to the type of man who worked there. How old Cleveland was at this time is not known, but the age of Captain Comer is known precisely. He was, as a matter of fact, getting a little elderly for fisticuffs, being 45 years of age. A complete sketch of his life is given in "New London Whaling Captains", by Bernard L. Colby, published by the Marine Historical Association of Mystic, Connecticut, whom I wish to thank for the information. George Comer was born at Quebec in 1858, of parents who came from England, and lived in Connecticut from his childhood. Practically all his seafaring life was spent in whalers, his first being the *Nile* in 1875 and the best-known probably being the *Canton* of New Bedford in which he sailed as second mate. The *Era* had been visiting Hudson's Bay almost since she had been built and it was this ship, under a very well-known American whaling master called J. O. Spicer, which killed a whale believed by some to be the biggest ever caught. It was said to be 125 feet long with jawbones of 18 feet and as its skeleton was assembled at a museum at Old Mystic the figures should be correct. But if they are, this whale was certainly a monster, for nothing like the length of 125 feet is mentioned by any authority, for any type of whale. Even the blue whale, "the largest and most powerful mammal in the world", as it has been described, does not exceed a length of 100 feet and it was certainly no blue whale which the *Era* caught. Captain Comer and the *Era* are mentioned more than once in the "Arctic Pilot", Vol. 3, where it is stated that the Canadian Government vessel *Neptune* and the *Era* wintered at Fullerton Harbour, at the south end of Roe's Welcome, in 1903/04, which is when Captain Murray wintered at Repulse Bay. Captain Comer's name is perpetuated in the region by Comer Strait, at the north end of Southampton Island. He was still alive in 1936 aged 78, being then the "only living whaling captain in Connecticut".

On 23rd July 1904, the *Active* arrived back at Repulse Bay and made fast to a floe at Beach Point, the southern entrance to the bay. Captain Murray had killed one whale that spring and another was killed during the summer. The *Active* left for home again on 13th September, taking Captain Murray with her. He had handed over the *Ernest William* to another master who had come out in the *Active* and was going home for a holiday. He tells us that "we dropped anchor near Cary's Swan Nest on Coats Island and allowed the Eskimos ashore to get a few deer for their winter clothing. At 8 p.m. they arrived back, having got quite a number of deer and bear". It is now more than sixty years since Captain Murray was at Coats Island in the *Active*, and yet more than forty years later the island was still not surveyed and charts of 1947 give the north coast in dotted lines. On the other hand, there has been a lighthouse on the island, at Cary's Swan Nest, for many years, something unknown throughout the area in Captain Murray's day. Coats Island was made into a reindeer reserve in 1920, as was Southampton Island. From Coats Island the *Active* went to Ashe Inlet, in Hudson Strait, anchoring in Lake Harbour on 23rd September. She left for home on 29th September and arrived at Dundee on 20th October 1904, a passage of 21 days. Her cargo from the Arctic included 2 whales, 69 white whales, 38 walrus, 52 seals, 32 bears, 157 fox, 30 musk ox and 15 tons of mica.

CHAPTER EIGHT

THE "ERNEST WILLIAM"

ON 10th June, 1905, Captain Murray again went out in the *Active* to take over the *Ernest William*. On the 22nd June the *Active* was beset in ice and did not reach Resolution Island, at the entrance to Hudson Strait, until 1st July. It was then that she had a real mishap. She had finally found clear water near East Bluff, at the south-east corner of Meta Incognita, when the propeller struck a piece of ice and broke the tail shaft, and from then on she was a sailing vessel. On the 5th, she was so badly nipped abreast the port bunker that the crew got their gear on deck thinking she would break up, but the pressure eased and she escaped. It happened again the next day, but again she escaped damage or worse. There was a particularly good example here, of the disadvantages a sailing vessel worked under, compared with a steamer; for experiencing nothing but calms and light winds it took the *Active* no less than 28 days to cover the 300 miles from where she smashed her tail shaft to Lake Harbour, in Hudson Strait. As Captain Murray remarked: "It had taken us about a month to do a thirty-hour sail". The only means of progress was to heave her through the ice with the steam winch and using the whale lines for this purpose, many of them were worn out. Whale lines cost money and with nearly a month of the all-too-short whaling season lost, such incidents as this were particularly exasperating at a time when Scottish whalers were finding it hard to make a profit at all.

Prospects for reaching Repulse Bay, on the other side of Hudson Bay, nearly 700 miles away, seemed practically non-existent unless repairs to the tail shaft could be effected and it was decided to beach the *Active* at Lake Harbour for an attempt to be made. Explosives were used to blast a way through the ice to a suitable place on the beach and the vessel was put ashore stern-first. It was then found that the tail shaft was broken near the propeller boss. It would have required a jack to take off the screw, so it and the outer section of the shaft were drawn out and hove on board and the inner portion of the shaft drawn into the tiny engine-room and the aperture plugged. The vessel was then put afloat again. The chief engineer had to admit that he could see no way of effecting a repair without equipment which was not available and it was Captain Murray who suggested the means by which the shaft was re-united and the vessel, once more, able to use her engines. Captain Murray said that "it would take too long to describe how the shaft was repaired, but I managed it. We commenced repairs on 1st August, and finished on the 8th, but could not beach the vessel again because of the ice until the 14th. On that day we ran our shaft out and shipped the propeller, hauled off again and sailed the following morning with all our natives on board".

On 19th August the *Active* anchored in Port de Boucherville, at the eastern end of Nottingham Island. That day 38 walrusses and one polar bear were killed and the crew was employed in salting down walrus hides. Leaving Port de Boucherville the barque was aground on a reef for a short time but soon got afloat again. The place had been used as an observation station for a Government expedition back in 1884, but in spite of this Nottingham Island, had not been fully surveyed, even in 1947 and charts of the area still show the coast, as a dotted line. On the 20th, steaming along the coast of Coats Island, eight polar bears were seen on the beach. On the 24th she anchored near the *Ernest William* in Repulse Bay, the American schooner *Era* with Captain Comer aboard also being there. The *Era* had captured eight whales, the *Ernest William* two, since whaling commenced in the Spring. The stores brought out by the *Active* were exchanged for the ketch's Arctic produce and then Captain Murray took over the *Ernest William* and was towed by the *Active*, right up into Lyon Inlet, in the southern part of the Melville Peninsular, where he had decided to winter. Captain Parry had wintered there with

H.M.S. *Hecla* and H.M.S. *Fury*, in 1821, and Lyon Inlet is named after Lieutenant Lyon R.N. who accompanied Parry, and Captain Murray was the first man to winter there since Parry.

The first job at Lyon Inlet was to beach the *Ernest William* for repairs to her bottom. On 11th September, the *Active* hove up her anchor and set off for Dundee, leaving Captain Murray with a carpenter, a cook, one sailor and about 45 Eskimo men with their families. He records: "We gave her three cheers, as it was probably the last we should see of any vessel until the following year. That day we sighted one whale, which one of my Eskimo boat-steerers darted and missed".

It was November 1st before the *Ernest William* was properly frozen-in and for some time before that "we had a very anxious time, as the ice kept breaking up and several times the ketch was almost pushed on the beach". Captain Murray goes on to tell us: "The same night, a bear came close to the Eskimo huts and Muckputaa, a Nichilik, rushed out of the house and when quite close to the bear, fired at it, but his rifle failed to go off. The bear sprang at him and knocked him down and he was badly clawed across his forehead and cheeks, his back torn over his shoulder blades and his left wrist and hand badly bitten. We got him doctored up and he was well again in a week or two. On 6th November we could hear a bear walking around on the ice close to the ship but it was too dark to see him. On 15th November I sent a sled to Igloolik on a trading expedition and they returned on 16th February, three months later, with a few bear and fox skins". Igloolik is an island in Fury and Hecla Straits, off the north end of the Melville Peninsular.

Eskimos are stoics where pain is concerned and on one occasion Captain Murray found an Eskimo woman picking pus out of a carbuncle on her husband's body with a bent wire. His method of dealing with this carbuncle was a somewhat original but completely successful one. Putting some blubber in a basin he let the sun melt it and then mixing it with carbolic acid, applied it to the wound, which quickly healed, helped no doubt by the pure air of the Arctic. He often had to act as dentist and with no anaesthetics to kill the pain used to press on each side of the head, the effect being to numb the mouth and thus deaden the nerves.

Cannibalism was not unknown among Eskimos when driven to it by starvation, although there was no known case of a person being killed for the food their body would provide; it was only practised when a person had already died, usually from starvation. In the 80's and 90's, when there was much starvation among the natives in the Wager Inlet area, there was a good deal of cannibalism. Captain Murray never came across a case of it, but during that winter at Lyon Inlet, met an Eskimo woman from Igloolik who told him she had once been driven to it. She was on a journey with her husband from Pond Inlet, North end of Baffin Island, to Igloolik when they encountered soft snow which greatly retarded them. Running out of food, the husband went off to try and shoot something, leaving the woman in an igloo with her two young children. The husband never returned, having presumably been injured in some mishap and died of starvation, so the woman was left alone with her children and no food. First one child died and was buried in the snow, then the other, and eventually, when nearly dead from hunger, she ate both her children. Later she was found by other Eskimos, who looked after her, and when Captain Murray talked with her she was a strong healthy woman. In Dr. D. M. Lindsay's book "A Voyage to the Arctic in the Whaler *Aurora*", he mentions an interesting legend about cannibalism among settlers in East Greenland, who had gone there from Norway. According to this, the colonists became eaters of human flesh and grew to like it; but as these people have not been heard of since 1408, the legend remains just a legend.

During that winter they had an unexpected visitor in the person of Sergeant Edginton, of the Royal North West Mounted Police (it had received the prefix of 'Royal' the previous year, in June 1904), who had an interpreter and a dog driver with him. In those days, with no link with the outside world once winter had shut down, such a visitor coming unheralded must have been very welcome. So much have wireless and the aeroplane become part of our lives today, that it is difficult to imagine men completely shut off from human contacts as they were aboard the *Ernest William*, in 1905.

Winter Island, near Lyon Inlet, being the place where Parry had wintered in 1821, Captain Murray asked the Eskimos who went over there sealing, to bring back any curios they might come across, as probably no European foot had trodden that island in all the years since Parry was there. One of the Eskimos took him rather too literally, and came back with a gravestone on which was the name Elder, described as "ice master", the man with knowledge of Arctic conditions who would be in charge of navigating through the ice. Captain Murray saw to it that the stone was returned to the grave.

The summer of 1906, was a particularly unlucky one for Arctic Whalers, owing to the prevalence of south-easterly gales, which packed the ice to such an extent, that the ships could not reach the whaling grounds. This state of affairs prevailed also on the other side of America, in the Bering Sea, as we are told in Captain A. J. Cook's book "Pursuing the Whale". He was at that time master of the steam whaling barque *Bowhead*, caught in the ice at Herschel Island together with a number of other whalers. But his worries were not confined to his ship being jammed in the ice, for his wife had a nervous breakdown as a result of her privations and his crew mutinied and he eventually left the *Bowhead*, still jammed in the ice and returned to San Francisco. So tightly packed in the ice was the *Ernest William*, that she was unable to get out of Lyon Inlet to go to Repulse Bay, where it had been planned she should rendezvous with the *Active*. On five occasions that summer, whales were heard blowing but because of the pack ice, the boats could not get off the beach and not a whale was caught. It would almost seem that Captain Murray was discouraged by the poor results of his winter in Lyon Inlet, for he tells us that "on 8th September gave up hopes of getting the vessel out to reach the store ship lying in Repulse Bay. I was not inclined to have another winter in these quarters. On 7th September we could see smoke from a fire on the west side of the Inlet, so got a boat out and worked up the Inlet between the pack ice and the land to the west shore and spoke to the Eskimos we found there. They told us the store ship (the *Active*), was lying in Repulse Bay, and gave me a letter from the captain". This letter, from his brother, the captain of the

Active, told him that a relief was waiting for him aboard that ship, but as the *Ernest William* was locked in the ice at Lyon Inlet, it meant he would have to go overland to the *Active*, which he proceeded to do. His trip to Repulse Bay gives one an idea of the real hardships any man who elected to live in the Arctic had to accept in those days.

"We started off for the head of Lyon Inlet with four boats. It took us two days before we reached the head of the inlet where we put the boats up on the land and divided our effects among the Eskimos and ourselves for carrying. Before we started off I explained to the Eskimos that as we had no cooking utensils and no tent, each man would have to carry his own food, so each one took some hard bread (biscuit), boiled deer meat and salt pork and we set off on our journey by land to Repulse Bay". (The distance in a straight line was about fifty miles, but considerably more by the route round the head of the inlet). "After climbing the high land we had to wade two rivers, so everyone was pretty well soaked. When it came in dark we looked round for somewhere to sleep and the Eskimos built little bits of shelter with stones and turf for themselves. Fortunately, one of them had a piece of canvas about four feet square, which we used for covering some of the bundles. I managed to get my head under the canvas among the bundles but the rest of my body was exposed to the rain. The other three white men did the same and we lay there waiting for daylight, so we could make a start. Being under cover it was impossible to have a smoke which might have helped the time to pass quicker. As soon as it was light enough to see to walk, we started off again. It was still raining but fortunately not so heavily, and soon after daylight the rain ceased. Late in the evening of 11th September, two Eskimos and myself reached Haviland Bay (a large bight in the north-east corner of Repulse Bay), and there found an old whaleboat belonging to an Eskimo. We looked round and found the mast and sail and oars buried and covered with stones and by the time the boat had been rigged, some of the others had arrived. We could see a fire in the distance, so set off in the boat and reached the *Active* late that night. Mr. Cleveland, an American whom I had recommended as a good man, to take my place, had come out to relieve me (the man who had had the fight with Captain Comer), and the following day, he and his men and the Eskimos I had brought over, started on the journey back to the ketch, which I had left, in the charge of a few Eskimos''. Cleveland later worked for the Hudson's Bay Company and died many years ago.

On rejoining the *Active*, Captain Murray, learned that on her passage home the previous year, the ship had encountered a strong easterly gale in Davis Straits, had lost her propellor through the engine racing, and as a result completed the voyage home as a sailing ship. But the tail end shaft which he had been instrumental in repairing had withstood all the considerable strain put upon it and on arrival at Dundee had been placed on the jetty for shore engineers to examine the repair, made under such difficult conditions. The *Active* left Repulse Bay on 14th September, and again called in at Port de Boucherville to let her Eskimos go deer-hunting for food and skins for their winter clothing. On 7th October, she left Lake Harbour and arrived back in Dundee, at the end of October (1906). There had been good years and bad years at the fishing, but 1906 must have been, one of the worst on record, for the *Scotia*, Captain Robertson, was the only ship to bring back any whales, four small ones being caught east of Greenland.

The following year, 1907, John Murray served as Mate aboard the steam barque, *Scotia*, under Captain Robertson, universally known as "caffee Tam", because of his prejudice against strong drink. The *Scotia*, a vessel of 357 gross tons, had been built at Drammen, Norway, in 1872, as the *Hekla*, and became one of the Scottish whaling fleet in 1902. Of the eight square-rigged whalers in which Captain Murray served, the *Scotia*, was one of the only two fitted with double topsails, the other being the *Esquimaux*. All the rest had single topsails fitted with Cunningham's patent reefing gear. Double topsails came into vogue back in the sixties and quickly replaced single topsails because of the ease of handling them with fewer men. But although easier to handle, a good deal of sail area was lost with double topsails and the single variety was retained in whalers because they carried much larger crews, which could easily manage the big sails. There was another reason, too, and this was that when forcing a passage through the ice, every inch of canvas was of value. On the other hand, few of the whalers carried anything above their very big single top-gallants, the explanation of this being that when a vessel was whaling, perhaps with all her boats out, the few men left on board would have been unable to handle a heavily-rigged craft.

In the *Scotia*, John made a voyage to the Greenland Sea, calling in at Lerwick first, to pick up extra men as had been the custom in the whalers for many years in the ships which were not wintering in the Arctic. There were two passengers, a Mr. Kinnear, an ornithologist, and Mr. Mossman, a meteorologist. In the Greenland Sea, the *Scotia*, killed two large whales but lost a third, after no less than 19 lines had been planted in it. From the Greenland Sea, she went on to Davis Straits, calling in at Reykjavik for bunkers, and it was at the Icelandic port that there occurred a series of incidents which must have strengthened Captain Robertson's already strong views about the evils of drink. Someone from the shore brought to the ship, bottles of corn brandy, which was traded with the crew, for tins of meat, the result being chaos. For the crew, once they had partaken of the fiery liquid, went mad and took complete charge of the ship. On the poop, lashed to the mizzen mast because it was too large to be stowed below, was a barrel of porter and once the corn brandy had done its work, the men brought along their pannikins and helped themselves. One man, demented with drink, went aloft and Captain Murray, fearing for his safety, followed him. The man reached the upper topsail yard, ran out along it and dived off ino Reykjavik Harbour, sixty feet below. He ought to have been either drowned or killed, but the Lord looks after drunken men—sometimes—and he was fished out, little the worse for his mad act. There were fights galore and two men had to be taken to hospital, one of them with a suspected fracture of the jaw. Two others were put in jail and brought back aboard, when the ship left for Davis Straits. The two scientists left the ship at Reykjavik, apparently having had enough of life aboard a whaler after the ugly affair of the corn brandy. Two other passengers took their place, a missionary called Bielby and an Eskimo woman.

The gloom which must have hung over the ship after the Reykjavik affair was not lightened by any good luck from then on, for the *Scotia* killed no more whales that voyage, and arrived back in Dundee with only the two killed in the Greenland Sea. The *Diana*, another auxiliary barque, accounted for one in Davis Straits and these three were the total for the year. This year saw the end of the little *Windward*, in which Captain Murray had made his first voyage to sea in 1884. She was wrecked on June 25th, near the Cary Islands, in Smith Sound, off the west coast of Greenland, in 77 N., which is less than a thousand miles from the Pole. Her crew had a grim time of it in the boats before being rescued by the *Morning*, on July 6th, two men dying of exposure after being rescued. She was 47 years old when wrecked.

From 1908 to 1911, inclusive, Captain Murray commanded the *Balaena*, a steam whaling barque of 416 gross tons. Like the *Scotia*, she had been built in Drammen in 1872, as the *Mjolner* and came under the British flag about 1890. At the time he had her, she was owned by the Balaena Fishing Company, of which J. M. Mitchell, was the managing owner. In 1892, the *Balaena*, had been one of the four ships sent from Dundee to the Antarctica, in search of the right whale reported by Ross, in 1842, as being present in large numbers there. We have a spirited and light-hearted account of the *Balaena*'s Antarctic voyage in W. G. Burn Murdoch's book "From Edinburgh to the Antarctic". He tells us that the *Balaena*, was a "pet ship", built to the ideas of her Norwegian master. "Her sides, with timbers and linings 32 inches thick, are supported in every direction by huge beams and natural knees. The focsle is for'd below the main deck. Aft, the deck house roof rises about two feet above the poop, leaving a narrow alleyway round the stern. Her sheer is greater than in British ships and her lines are somewhat after those of the Viking ships". She was called the *Balaena*, from the latin name of the right or bowhead whale, Balaena Mysticetus, which has been used as a name for whalers for many years. There was a *Balaena*, hailing from Lynn, or King's Lynn, at the whaling in 1789, and

"BALAENA"

another one, an auxiliary, barque built at San Francisco in 1883, was wrecked in 1901.

Captain Murray's first voyage in the *Balaena*, started with a tragedy. Soon after leaving Dundee a sailor committed suicide by jumping overboard and although a boat was lowered, no trace of him was found. The day of the Scottish whalers was now nearly over and yet, right at the end of their history, Captain Murray was among the most successful of the whaling captains. A return issued by the owners of the *Balaena*, James Mitchell, in 1908, shows that Captain Murray in the *Balaena*, caught 4 whales, while Captain Robertson in the *Scotia*, got 6.

"BALAENA"

The following year, 1909, Captain Murray again killed 4 whales and in 1910, five. He told me that the 1909 voyage gave a return of 33 and one third per cent for the money invested. The year 1908, may be taken as a significant one in the history of the old-time whalers, for Captain John A. Cook, in his book "Pursuing the Whale" tells us that 1908 was the last year in which the American whalers out of San Francisco went north to the Bering Sea after whales. He says that bone "sold as low as two dollars a pound and very small quantities were wanted at that price. This meant a losing business, for at that price, the cost of outfitting and maintaining the vessels could not be met". Two dollars a pound for bone is £930 a ton, which although poor compared to the £3,000 per ton given by Lubbock as the price in 1906, was still not a negligible sum. In spite of what Captain Cook said, whaling must still have been a paying game, for otherwise there is no explanation of why he would have had a whaler built for him in 1910. She was the *Viola*, a brigantine, built at Essex, Mass., and until she went missing in 1918, was an extremely profitable investment. But her quarry was the sperm whale, or cachalot, a toothed whale hunted for its sperm oil, not the, by now nearly extinct right whale.

It was during his time in the *Balaena*, that Captain Murray reached his furthest north, 82, 20, which is in Kennedy Channel, between North-west Greenland and Grinnel Land. He could have gone further, but in his own words "as I was looking for whales and not going to the north pole, I turned back". Fury Beach, in Prince Regent Inlet, hundreds of miles to the south and west of Captain Murray's furthest north, has been described as "classic ground in the annals of Arctic adventure", but the area to which Captain Murray reached in the *Balaena*, could safely be given the same title, for it is thickly sprinkled with names connected with the conquest of the North: Kane Basin, Cape Beechey, Scoresby Bay, Lady Franklin Sound, Nares Land. Right up there on top of the world there is an island named after one John Murray, and if it is not named after the John Murray whose biography this is, then there is a rather remarkable coincidence, since John Murray Island is in the same latitude as that which Captain Murray told me was his furthest north. In telling me of the position which he had reached he made no mention of any island bearing his name, but this could be easily explained by the fact that he was the most modest man I have met, apparently incapable of "blowing his own trumpet", on even the quietest of notes. It was his ambition to make the North-West passage from east to west, but the opportunity to attempt it never came his way. By temperament, physical qualities and experience he would have been the ideal man for such a demanding challenge.

In 1911, during the winter lay-up of the *Balaena*, Captain Murray made a voyage as mate of the steamer *Glenisla*, another of the ships owned by James Mitchell. This took him out to Cartagena, with coal and home from Oran, North Africa, with esparto grass. At the end of this voyage he was offered the command of another of Mitchell's steamers but in spite of the depressed state of whaling, elected to stay in the ships he had known all his life. He was now 42, no longer a young man, and the fact that he turned down an offer which would almost certainly have provided him with a more secure future than the Arctic could provide seems to indicate that his heart was in the north.

CHAPTER NINE

THE "ALBERT" AND THE WAR YEARS

IN April 1912 he took over the ketch *Albert* for a whaling voyage to the Greenland sea, and with Scottish whaling, all but finished had difficulty getting hold of a good crew. There were still harpooners available but the rest of the crew was, what he described as a "mixed lot". As required by law he gave his new men a month's advance of wages when signing-on but as they were mostly strangers to him, he was rather doubtful if they would show up for sailing and asked the police to keep an eye on them. With not a single whaler of any size now owned in Peterhead the Sailors' Foy was now a thing of the past, but even so, his men kept up the spirit of it; and although all hands were aboard at sailing time, some of them joined with practically no outfit, having pawned everything pawnable for the wherewithal to quench their thirst.

The *Albert* was in her way a famous little vessel. She had been built at Great Yarmouth by H. Fellows & Son in 1889 for the Mission to Deep Sea Fishermen, to patrol the North Sea and for three years gave wonderful service to the fishermen. Then, in 1892, she went out to Labrador with a young man on board who, was later to become, more famous than her. This was Wilfred Grenfell, eventually Sir Wilfred Grenfell, whose name will always be associated with Labrador. He tells us that her freeboard, being only three feet, he replaced her wooden hatches with iron ones and sheathed her for'd along the water line with greenheart; for running, a large square sail was fitted on the foremast. The one fault with the *Albert* was that she was too large for her ketch rig, and as a result was under-canvassed. This must have been an irritation to Captain Murray, used to adequately rigged vessels. She had a gross tonnage of 155 and there were plenty of vessels of this tonnage rigged as three-masted schooners. It is a striking thought that Captain Murray's first command, the barque-rigged *Perseverance*, was only 24 tons larger than the ketch-rigged *Albert* and one foot longer. In 1912 the *Albert* was owned by the Albert Whaling Company, with W. H. Leask as manager, and was their largest vessel.

Almost from the start, this voyage did not go well. It was soon found that with the boats swung out, ready for whaling the vessel worked very badly under sail, and on May 7th she received a blow from the ice which caused her to leak. From then on the pumps were constantly manned and with the weather very cold there was difficulty keeping them free of ice. To try and stop the leak, which was for'd, the ceiling, or light inner planking, was removed and the space between the frames filled with black varnish and oakum, but this had no effect. Finding a patch of water free, from ice, casks were then filled with water and placed aft, to lift her head and get at the leak from the outside, but this also failed. Then the old and often successful trick of feeding the leak with chopped oakum and sawdust was tried, the idea being that the suction caused by the water flowing into the leak, would draw in the oakum and sawdust and stop the leak. This also proved ineffectual. The carpenter then started to build a bulkhead to confine the water to the fore part and an attempt was made to reach the land at Spitzbergen, to beach the *Albert*, but there was too much ice for this to be done. Accordingly, Captain Murray set off for the whaling grounds again, hopeful that the leak would take up, but instead it got worse and the ketch was making sixteen inches of water in an hour. To continue whaling was hopeless, for even if they had seen a whale the crew was constantly at the pumps and a boat could not have been manned. So another attempt was made to reach the land and this time the vessel was able to work through the ice and was beached at Safety Harbour, Spitzbergen. Again casks filled with water, were stowed aft, to try and raise her head, but with only a small range of tide the full extent of the leak could not be uncovered. A freshwater tank was cut up and the plating was bent round the forefoot and after all possible had been done they set off once more to look for whales. But the *Albert* was still leaking, so without more ado Captain Murray decided it was useless to carry on and set off back to Peterhead, where he arrived on June 10th. The crew about which he had doubts when he signed them on, had shown up very well on this unfortunate voyage and Captain Murray remarked: "I would like here, to give praise to my crew; they were all fine workers, especially the carpenter".

After the *Albert* had been drydocked and repaired at Peterhead, the owner suggested that she should make, a wintering voyage and accordingly Captain Murray set off once more, on 9th July (1912), this time for Hudson's Bay. He arrived in Repulse Bay on 1st September and on 14th took aboard his Eskimos and their families, intending to go to the Ottawa Islands, lying over on the east side of Hudson's Bay, to winter there. North of the Wager River, in Roe's Welcome, however, the ice was found to be impassible, so the *Albert* was turned round and ran back before the wind to Repulse Bay, the ice fast closing in on the land as she did so. Whales having been seen there, Captain Murray changed his plans and wintered in the locality he had known so well in earlier years. The *Platina*, which had wintered with him, in the same place in 1896/97, also spent the winter in Repulse Bay. She was now 65 years old.

On 10th October, the vessel was frozen in and the *Albert*'s crew settled down to the long Arctic winter. She was in 66° North latitude, so at noon on December 31st, the sun was just on the horizon. During the winter, two sledges were sent up towards King William's Island and two others to Igloolik, in Foxe Channel, to trade with the Eskimos there, Captain Murray hoping in this way, to obtain some Arctic produce to offset the expense of the voyage, as he was not hopeful of getting any whales. On 24th May, Mr. Jamieson the mate, died after a long illness and was buried in a cairn on the mainland.

The summer of 1913 was a poor one for whaling in Repulse Bay, pack ice reducing the opportunities for cruising, but on 15th August, one large whale was killed. On 4th September, the *Albert* left Repulse Bay on the first stage of her journey home, and on the 10th spoke the Hudson's Bay Company's auxiliary barque *Pelican* and received some mail from her, the first they had had since leaving Peterhead more than a year before. The *Pelican* was an interesting old ship, having been built at Devonport, in 1877, as H.M.S. *Pelican*, a masted warship which served mostly on the Pacific and North American stations until she was sold out of the Service in 1901. Peterhead was reached on 4th October. That winter of 1912-13, was the tenth Captain Murray had spent, in the Arctic and was to be his last.

Of the year 1913, Norman and Fraser's book "Giant Fishes, Whales and Dolphins" has this to say: "The final reports make sad reading: Harmer says 'Only one ship left Dundee in 1912, and 1913 and . . . the total catch in each of those two years was returned as O'. So ended a fishery which at one time used to send 200 to 300 ships a year northward from British ports alone".

The owners of the *Albert*, apparently satisfied with the returns they were getting, wanted Captain Murray to take out the ketch again the following season, but this he declined to do, without an engine being fitted. Messrs. Kinnes were still the owners of the steam whaling barque *Active*, in which he had sailed as mate with his brother in 1898. In November 1913, this brother Captain Alex Murray, had died aboard the *Active* whilst in winter quarters, at the Ottawa Islands and in this way it came about that his younger brother took command of the vessel the following year. Captain Alex Murray had commanded the *Active*, for no less than 15 years.

The *Active*, with Captain John Murray in command, left Dundee on 8th June, 1914, bound for Hudson Bay, the steam whaling barque *Morning*, Captain F. Fairweather, leaving the same day bound for Davis Straits. The *Morning*, also owned by R. Kinnes, had been built at Tonsberg in 1871, as the *Morgenen*, and was slightly bigger than the *Active*. She had become well-known back in 1902, when she went to the relief of the *Discovery*, in the Antarctic and it was after this that she became one of Kinnes' fleet. It was a significant date, that 8th June 1914, for it marked the last occasion when whalers of the old type left a British port on a whaling cruise. They did not know when they left Dundee, that before they returned, the country would be plunged into a war of undreamed-of magnitude. On 23rd July, the *Active* was at Whale Point, on the west side of Hudson's Bay, having gone their to pick up Eskimos to man the whaleboats. The next day, at Fullerton Harbour, Captain Murray found some old friends among the Eskimos, and having taken them aboard, set out for the Ottawa Islands, on the other side of Hudson Bay, which by this time, had come to be regarded as a good place for whaling. The ice preventing them making easting, Captain Murray anchored off Coats Island, near Southampton Island, and allowed his Eskimos to go ashore, hunting deer of which they shot enough, to keep them in food for a long time. On the same day, no less than twelve bears were shot.

On 17th August, the *Active*, anchored in Murray Harbour, Gilmour Island (one of the Ottawa group), named after Captain Alex Murray, who had died there, the previous year. When they arrived, three bears and an Eskimo dog were seen feeding on whalemeat on the beach, but though a boat was lowered to go in chase, the bears, escaped. The dog was brought aboard and proved to be one of a pair, that had escaped from the *Active*, the previous year. Captain Murray visited the grave of his brother on Gilmour Island, and also that of a harpooner, who had died about the same time.

It would have been fitting if what was to be, the very last whaling voyage of the *Active* had been a successful one; but although conditions were extremely good and the boats were out every day from 17th August to 25th September, not a single whale was even seen, although one was heard blowing. On 1st September, the schooner *Laddie*, of St. John's N.F.L., arrived with Captain Harold Bartlett in command and two passengers, Mr. R. G. Flaherty and a French-Canadian, Jean Laduc, who were on a prospecting expedition. Mr. Flaherty, who was later to become well-known in the film industry, had with him a motion picture camera, and took photos of the *Active*'s Eskimos playing their traditional games, but unfortunately, these films were later destroyed in a fire aboard the *Laddie*.

On 29th September, the *Active*, left Southampton Island, where she had paid off her Eskimos, and arrived at Lake

Harbour, Hudson Straits, on 4th October. There the Hudson's Bay Company's launch *Darrell*, with a Mr. Lee on board, passed close to them and shouted across, that Britain was at war with Germany. This was their first intimation of the war that was to change history. The *Active* left for home on 8th October and Captain Murray tells us that "on the 24th, a large British cruiser appeared out of the haze, and we were doubtful at first whether it was a British or a German vessel until we sighted the White Ensign. We flag-waved them and asked if the war was over and got the answer, 'No, just started'. The following night another British cruiser played her searchlight on us and we tried them by morse but got no reply. Off Dunnet Head, we were stopped by two British cruisers and were boarded by two officers, who overhauled our papers and gave me sailing directions. On 28th October, we arrived at Dundee. Quite a number of the crew being naval reserve men, they were allowed forty-eight hours' leave before joining up. So endeth the unfortunate voyage of 1914, which was the last of the Dundee whaling".

CHAPTER TEN

THE WAR YEARS

THE years from 1915 to 1919, Captain Murray spent in his former command the *Albert*, now fitted with an auxiliary engine but still with her inadequate ketch rig. He took her over from Captain W. F. Milne, another well-known whaling master, who commanded the famous whaler *Eclipse* from 1893 until she was sold to Norway in 1909. Captain Milne had had with him as mate in the *Albert* another whaling personality in the person of William Adams, known as "Young Adams" to distinguish him from his father, the famous whaling master who had commanded Scottish whalers for twenty years, killed close on 200 whales and is described by Basil Lubbock as "one of the most successful of the latter-day whaling masters, as well as one of the most popular".

The *Albert* was now owned by the Arctic Gold Exploration Company and the story of how this change of ownership came about makes interesting reading, for it has about it the ingredients of the traditional hidden treasure story. It is given to us by H. T. Munn, a director of the Arctic Gold Company, in his book "Prairie Trails and Arctic By-Ways". At some date in the 1860's the cooper of an un-named Scottish whaler landed at a place in Baffin Land with a boat's crew in search of water and quite by accident came across two small nuggets of gold. These he later sold to a jeweller in Dundee. Later still, when he was dying, he gave a chart he had made of the spot where he had found the gold to a storekeeper in St. John's N.F.L. who had befriended him (how these treasure stories follow a faithful pattern!) and this man eventually gave it to George Bartlett, a member of a famous Newfoundland family of seafarers. H. T. Munn heard the story from George Bartlett at about the time that a man called Robert S. Janes arrived in Toronto claiming that he too had found placer gold in Baffin Land. Thinking that the story was worth investigating, H. T. Munn chartered the sealer *Algerine* (another former British warship) with Captain John Bartlett in command and went up Davis Straits to try and find the place marked on the old cooper's chart. Having reached a point near where he believed the gold had been found, Munn left the *Algerine* and set off to look for it, but failed to find anything. He returned to where he had left the *Algerine* to learn that only a few hours after his departure, she had been nipped in the ice and sank in twenty minutes. The date of the loss was 16th July 1912 and the place, four miles off Cape Weld, in Ponds Inlet. Her crew had taken to their boats and gone to Button Point, in Ponds Inlet, in 32 north, where Munn later found them. They were saved from a winter in the Arctic by the arrival of the Newfoundland sealer *Neptune*, which had brought a party of prospectors with the man Janes, whose story of having found gold in Baffin Land, had partly inspired H. T. Munn to charter the *Algerine*. The day after the *Neptune*'s arrival Janes was taken ashore by those who had financed the *Neptune* expedition and told to lead them, to where he had claimed to have found the gold. They went to the Salmon River, which flows into Navy Board Inlet, near Lancaster Sound, but Janes was quite unable to find the place. He had been in a nervous state for some time, for at least one of the prospectors had doubted his story and threatened him that if he was lying he need expect no mercy. This man was so angry when Janes failed to show them where he had found the gold that he threatened to shoot him on the spot. Janes, thoroughly frightened, took off and ran for protection to Munn until the prospector's anger had subsided. An almost identical case, although on a much bigger scale, is related by J. Inches Thompson in his book "Voyages and Wanderings in Far Off Seas and Lands". The author was in New Zealand in 1861, when the discovery of gold at Gabriel's Gully set off many a stampede, some of which proved genuine, others false. A miner arrived in town one day with a quantity of gold and reported having struck it rich in the mountains. This set off a rush, but when the man was unable to show where he had got his gold, the angry miners were all for lynching him, or at least cutting off his ears and he was only saved by the intervention of the author's brother.

H. T. Munn and the crew of the *Algerine* returned to St. John's in the *Neptune* and although the voyage had been a complete failure for him, Munn decided that gold or no gold, there was money to be made by establishing trading posts in Baffin Land. In May 1914, he purchased the *Albert* as a supply ship for the trading posts and as already mentioned was fortunate enough to get Captain Milne to take charge of her, with "young" Adams as his mate. They left Peterhead for the Arctic on July 7th 1914, and after arrival at Button Point, Ponds Inlet, Munn left the *Albert* to establish a trading post and spend the winter there, the *Albert* returning to Peterhead.

It was on the outward passage of this voyage that the *Albert* put into Godhavn, Greenland, with engine trouble and while there Mr. Munn took photographs of a very famous little ship. This was the *Fox*, the vessel which in 1857 had been sent out by Lady Franklin to try to solve the mystery of the disappearance of her husband, Sir John Franklin, in the Arctic. Sir John had left England in 1845 with two ships, H.M.S. *Erebus* and H.M.S. *Terror*, to complete the discovery of the long-sought North West Passage. The last word of the two ships was when they spoke a whaler in Baffin Bay only two months after leaving England, and when more than two years had gone by with no word of them, the British Government sent out an expedition to find them. It failed to do so and from then on a number of other expeditions were sent out with no more success. In 1857 Lady Franklin, who had impoverished herself in her efforts to solve the mystery, bought the yacht *Fox*, built by Hall of Aberdeen two years earlier, and put Captain F. L. M'Clintock, R.N. (later Admiral Sir Leopold M'Clintock) in command. The *Fox* left Aberdeen in July 1857 and when she returned two years later, had established the fact that the two ships had been abandoned in April 1848, when they had already been beset in the ice in 70° N. 99° W. for nineteen months. Sir John Franklin had died in 1847 and of the 105 men who left the ships to try to reach the Hudson Bay not one survived. The object of the voyage had been achieved, however, and to the *Erebus* and *Terror* goes the honour of having discovered the North West Passage.

It seems a pity that no-one in Britain thought the *Fox* worth preserving, if only as a monument to the men of the *Erebus* and *Terror* whose lives were the price of the discovery; but no-one did so and in 1874 she was sold to owners in Denmark who were interested in the production of cryolite. Greenland is the main source of supply for this mineral, which is used for many industrial purposes, and for the next forty years, right up to 1914, the *Fox* was employed in the transport of cryolite from Greenland. The owners must have thought well of the little ship, for in 1893 they had another ship built for them in Denmark, a three-masted auxiliary schooner, which they called *Fox II*. Lady Franklin's *Fox* was broken up soon after H. T. Munn saw her.

Apparently Mr. Munn still hoped he might find gold where the old cooper said he had found it and after the break-up of the ice the following spring made a systematic search of every stream in the neighbourhood of the cooper's charted position but found no trace of gold. What he did find, however, were some lumps of yellow iron pyrites and came to the conclusion that this was what the old man had found and, with the passage of time, had deluded himself into believing was gold. It would make a good yarn in the pub of a night and after a few repetitions the old man would honestly believe it had been gold.

It was August 13th 1915, before the *Albert* showed up and Munn boarded her expecting to find "young" Adams in command, it having been arranged that he should take over from Captain Milne, who judging by Munn's book did not care for so small a command. Instead, he found Captain Murray, then a stranger to him, and heard with astonishment of the outbreak of war more than a year before. "Young" Adams had left the *Albert* when she got back to Peterhead and had gone piloting on the Home coast, and as already stated, it turned out that Captain Murray stayed in the *Albert* all through the war years. Mr. Munn soon found that, in his new captain, he had an outstanding man and in his book described him as "an exceedingly skilful and experienced ice-master as well as a most pleasant companion . . . he had an almost uncanny sense of ice navigation".

The *Albert* returned to Peterhead with Mr. Munn on board, arriving there after a good passage of 20 days. She left again on 22nd June 1916 and arrived at the trading post of Button Point on August 12th, ice conditions at the head of Baffin Bay being very bad, so that Mr. Munn wrote: "only Murray's skill in finding openings in the Middle Pack got us through". While the *Albert* was at Button Point, a Newfoundland sealer called the *Kite* came in, having on board the man Janes, who had misled so many people with his story of gold in Baffin Land. Janes was going to set up a trading station "somewhere in Eclipse Sound" (on the south-west side of Bylot Island).

After calling at Button Point the *Albert* took Mr. Munn right down the coast of Baffin Land to Durban Harbour, where a French Canadian called William Duval with his Eskimo wife and family and five other families, sixty dogs and a mass of equipment were taken aboard for passage into Hudson Bay. The *Albert* had a length of 100 feet and one marvels how such a conglomeration of men and women and squalling children, savage dogs, sledges and other Arctic gear were ever packed aboard that tiny vessel. They had a very rough passage into Hudson Bay, losing two boats, some of the dogs, all the food for the dogs, and some fishing nets. Eskimos, inured to hardship and danger from birth, are not nervous people, but even so are not impervious to fear, and many of them aboard the *Albert* on that stormy passage, crowded into the tiny focsle under almost unimaginable conditions, were both frightened and seasick. Mr. Munn mentions that Eskimos were the only people he had encountered who seemed amused at being seasick. Captain Murray was at this time 48 years of age, no longer a young man with the resiliency and buoyancy of youth, and to command a vessel like the *Albert* under such conditions called for qualities not only for professional skill, but also of self-restraint and patience possessed by few men.

It had been Mr. Munn's intention to put Duval ashore on either Coats Island or Southampton Island to start a trading post and go on himself to Repulse Bay to establish a post there. But it was late September when the *Albert* arrived at South

Bay, Southampton Island, and time for her to be setting off back to Peterhead if she was not to stay the winter in the Arctic, so Mr. Munn abandoned his plan for going to Repulse Bay and stayed with Duval at South Bay. William Duval must have been a wonderful man, for he was already nearly seventy, having first visited the Arctic in an American whaler fifty years earlier, in the 1860's. He told Munn that in his young days he had seen an Eskimo camp at Cape Dorset, on the southern coast of Foxe Land, Baffin Island, with 1000 Eskimos in it. And writing in 1932, Munn remarks that "that is about twice the total population of the whole of Baffin's Island today".

CHAPTER ELEVEN

A NEAR CALL

NOVEMBER 11th 1918, Armistice Day, found the *Albert*, at Halifax, N.S., Captain Murray having left her there to go home on leave. He rejoined for the voyage north the following year and left Halifax on June 28th 1919, for Ponds Inlet but had to put into St. John's N.F.L. with engine trouble on 6th July. Mr. Munn was again travelling in the ship. All through the war there had been difficulty getting men for the tiny *Albert*, and for part of the time she had a Russian chief and second engineer, a Swedish mate and a Norwegian cook. This voyage, there was a Swedish mate, called Lindberg, a very big powerful man, and a Swedish sailor named Hedland. Leaving St. John's on 11th July, the *Albert*, put into a small port on the Greenland coast above Godhavn (perhaps Upernavik), for water, and in allowing the crew to go ashore for a dance, broke a very strict Danish Government rule which forbade ships' crews to land in Greenland. This rule had been made necessary in the 19th century by the harm, physical and moral, done to the native inhabitants, by the crews of whalers, as a result of which the Eskimo population was rapidly decreasing.

1919, was a bad year for ice in Davis Straits and finding himself unable to make northing Captain Murray, made for a Company's post in Cumberland Gulf and it was not until 12th September that he came to an anchor off Button Point, Ponds Inlet. Later the *Albert*, went further into Ponds Inlet to a station, that the Arctic Gold Company had bought from Captain Bernier, where a French Canadian called Wilfred Caron was in charge. Caron had been in the Arctic for three years and was very glad to see them.

It was at this point that Robert S. Janes, once more comes

into the narrative. He had a trading station at Cape Crawfurd or Crawford, west of Cape Charles York in Lancaster Sound, in 74 North, and although it had been intended that the *Albert*, should call at Janes' station to pick up his Arctic produce, she had lost so much time because of bad ice conditions, that it could not be done before winter set in. Janes, like Caron, had been in the Arctic for three years and wanted to go south, and visited the *Albert*, at Bernier's station to arrange this, but without success. According to Mr. Munn, Janes was "a very difficult, unreasonable fellow . . . I offered to take him out but he refused, and as he started fighting with my man on deck, over some supplies, my man said he had sold him and which he had not paid for, Murray had to order him off the ship . . . the next day I renewed my offer, which he again refused . . . Janes said he was going out in the winter, by way of Foxe Channel and the west coast of Hudson Bay, a tremendous journey. I put an entry in my diary that day, that I did not think Janes would get out alive, for he had had a lot of trouble with the natives . . ." To talk about going overland from Lancaster Sound, in 74 north, even to Fort York, which was about the nearest settlement of any size at that time, in wintertime, seems wild talk, for the distance is at least 1,500 miles.

Captain Murray, did not have so much to say about Janes, but it was to the point: "He and our Managing Director, Mr. Munn, could not come to an agreement to take Mr. Janes and his produce home. Mr. Janes told me he would make the passage down to Hudson Bay by sledge and find a means of getting home. He and the Eskimos, did not seem to get along at all. Later in the fall, at Cape Crawford, the Eskimos shot him, giving him two bullets as Janes had often told them, one bullet would shoot an Eskimo, but it would take two to kill him. So the natives obliged him with two bullets". Mr. Munn's prophecy had come true.

Captain Murray's version of the murder of Janes was that following a quarrel over some furs Janes was trying to obtain from the Eskimos by barter, during which he threw a caribou head at Nookadloo's father, the son shot him. The account given in the book "The Royal Canadian Mounted Police", by L. Charles Douthwaite, to whom I am indebted, for the use of his

"NOOKADLOO"

material, is somewhat different: "Janes, who was consistently hard up, and generally unpopular with the natives, who seem to have been afraid of him, had been especially disliked by one Nookudlah, whose dogs he had threatened to shoot. Whereupon Nookudlah had called a meeting of the tribe, who decided unanimously that the white man must die before he had time to do any more harm. Assisted by Oorooeungnak and Ahteetah, Nookudlah, carried out the sentence forthwith".

The date of the murder was sometime in late 1919, but it was more than two years afterwards before justice overtook Nookudlah, in the person of Staff Sergeant (later Inspector), Joy of the Royal Canadian Mounted Police, after what is described in L. C. Douthwaite's book as "one of the most remarkable murder chases on record". Rumours of the murder of Janes had reached the police in 1921, and in the summer of that year, Staff Sergeant Joy arrived in Baffin Land to make investigations. In December (1921), he left Ponds Inlet, with a dog team and arrived at Cape Crawford 14 days later. There he disinterred the corpse of Janes and established the fact that he had been shot and then took the body 200 miles to Ponds Inlet where, as coroner, he held an inquest with a jury of three white traders. As a policeman in the famous force he was vested with various powers, among them those of a magistrate, and having issued a warrant for the arrest of the suspected murderers, set out to serve it. His mission took him to a remote settlement 500 miles away, where he arrested the three men and took them back to Ponds Inlet for trial. One succumbs to the temptation to use that overworked word "epic", to describe that journey, for an epic it certainly was, to travel 500 miles on foot in an Arctic midwinter and return with three suspected murderers. These three must have been docile enough prisoners, for Joy had no-one to help him guard them.

Back in Ponds Inlet, that tiny Arctic settlement, the full majesty of the law was brought to bear on the three suspects, with a judge, counsel for prosecution and defence, and full jury composed of ships' officers and traders. It seems probable that it would have been much easier (and cheaper!) to have taken the suspects south to where the law could have been administered in some city, but there were undoubtedly reasons for taking the mountain to Mahomet rather than the other way round. To an Eskimo, accustomed to kill off the newly born, in times of famine, and as has been shown earlier in this book, to witness or even assist in the suicide of the aged, the taking of human life was not a particularly serious thing, and it was felt that to impress upon the Eskimo mind the different attitude of the white man on the subject, the case should be tried in their own land, where all would know about it. Nookudlah was found guilty of the actual murder and sentenced to ten years' imprisonment in Stony Mountain Prison, Manitoba; Oorooeungnak was given two years' hard labour at the police post at Ponds Inlet and the third man, Ahteetah, was acquitted.

After serving part of his sentence in the grimly-named Stony Mountain Prison, Nookudlah was moved to a prison in Quebec, where, at the request of the police, Captain Murray saw him in 1927. In view of the man's poor state he advised that he should be sent back to his own part of the world and this was done, but Nookudlah died before his sentence was completed. A murderer he undoubtedly was, but one cannot help the feeling that it was only an evil combination of time and place and circumstance that made him one. There seems to be no doubt that Janes was unsuited to the lonely life of an Arctic trader, incapable of understanding the people, among whom he lived and upon whom he was dependent. Captain Murray's comment on the affair was that apart from Janes, he had never heard of a white man being attacked by Eskimos in all his years in the Arctic, and that if he were, it would be his own fault. This opinion was inspired by his regard for the Eskimo and was, no doubt, largely correct, but not entirely so. There had been the case of the two Roman Catholic priests, murdered at the appropriately named Bloody Falls, on the Coppermine River, in 1913/14, whose fate was not revealed until 1916, when the murderers, two Eskimos called Sinnisiak and Uluksak, were given life imprisonment, and it was in the course of the protracted and very costly investigations into the murders of Fathers Leroux and Rouvier that another dark Arctic mystery was uncovered. This was the case of two men named Radford and Street, who had disappeared back in 1912 and whose Eskimo murderers were not arrested until 1916. In this case also, the men were given life imprisonment.

With regard to the cases of "assisted suicide", or to give them their modern name, "mercy killings", these were very common in Captain Murray's day, and were apparently accepted by the authorities as an integral part of Eskimo life. But as was inevitable, there came a time when such practises could be no longer countenanced and they were brought to a halt, officially at any rate, in 1949, by a case having about it, some of the features attending the trial of Nookudlah, the killer of Janes. In that year a judge, jury, lawyers and other officials were flown 1,000 miles to Cambridge Bay, on the south coast of Victoria Island, in 69 North, 105 West, to try an Eskimo, Eeriykoot, for his part in the death of his mother, 45-year-old Nushakook, who was dying of tuberculosis and had begged him to help her kill herself, because she was in constant pain. At first he refused, saying he was "afraid of the white people", but later helped her to hang herself, his friend Ishakak helping. Eeriykoot, was found guilty of a reduced charge of assisting his mother to commit suicide and was given the nearly nominal sentence of having to remain at the police post at Cambridge Bay for one year. His friend Ishakak, was acquitted. The whole purpose of the trial was to impress upon the Eskimos that these "mercy killings", must stop.

On 20th September 1919, the *Albert*, sailed from Ponds Inlet and tried to work down the west side of Davis Straits, but finding the ice too heavy, turned back and followed the edge of the pack to the north. Captain Murray tells us that on 24th September, "entered the ice, to work through to the water on the east side. The young ice was forming fast among the heavier pack ice and sometimes the vessel was almost jammed. Had the wind fallen away, I fear we would have stuck in the ice, perhaps for the winter. Sitting up in the crow's nest, there were times when I had a twitching feeling in the pit of my stomach, for with no ammunition and with stores running short, I'm afraid the experience would have proved fatal for the crew. It was a glad sight when we reached the east water about 8 p.m. Stopped our engine, being very short of cylinder oil and sailed down the east shore of Davis Straits".

The following day they sighted the Devil's Thumb, a

remarkable pillar of rock, well-known to whalers, of which Lindsay in "A Voyage to the Arctic in the Whaler *Aurora*", remarks "Every one took off his hat to it as was the custom". On the 29th September, they ran into Godhavn, on Disko Island, Greenland, for water and to stow everything snugly for the run home across the stormy North Atlantic. Here they were hospitably entertained, by Governor Throne and his wife and Mr. Jensen, before setting off again. The crew wanted to have a dance and although this was against the rule forbidding crews of ships, to land in Greenland, the Governor shut his eyes to it and the dance was held. Various writers have spoken of the prettiness of the Greenland girls and one at least of the *Albert*'s crew was badly smitten. He was Wilfred Caron, the trader from Bernier's post, who was going to the U.K. in the ship.

Leaving Godhavn on 1st October, the *Albert*, at first made good headway down the Greenland coast before a moderate gale from NNW. On the 3rd, with the vessel labouring heavily, the throat halliards on the mainmast carried away and the big mainsail came down and was badly torn. After being repaired, the sail was hoisted again, but on the 9th, Captain Murray recorded that "the wind is light and right aft and the heavy mainsail flapping round, shaking the whole vessel and bursting the gear. Our whole trouble was that the vessel was too heavy, for the way she was rigged". Mr. Munn made a somewhat similar criticism when he wrote: "The ketch rig was unsuitable for a vessel of her size, owing to the weight of the mainsail, which was constantly carrying away something in a heavy seaway. I could not alter it satisfactorily, however". Photos of the *Albert*, show clearly the scanty rig and the very big space between the two masts.

Crossing the North Atlantic in the autumn, life was not easy for those aboard the little *Albert*, and on 7th October a bad leak gave cause for anxiety. On 12th, it was "blowing hard from the south-east, vessel rolling and pitching, busting up all our gear until she was almost a wreck aloft. On 13th October, the wind veered to the WSW with showers of snow, but being short of fuel oil for our engine, we were unable to haul the vessel head on to the sea. Vessel rolling and pitching a great deal, mainsail down for repairs. On the 17th, finished repairing our sails, vessel running before a strong NW gale with a small leg-of-mutton mainsail set".

The following day, 18th October, was to be one Captain Murray would remember for the rest of his life. He recorded that on that day, the wind was decreasing and a heavy sea running, and it was arranged that at 4 p.m., the vessel should be brought to the wind and the repaired mainsail bent on. The Swedish mate, Mr. Lindberg, was at the wheel, having sent the helmsman for'd to call all hands for the job of bending on the big sail, and Captain Murray, was standing aft talking to him, when without warning the *Albert*, shipped a tremendous sea, over the stern. For the mate, it was the end. One moment he was talking to Captain Murray, the next, he had been plucked from the wheel and overboard into eternity. It was not the end for the captain, but there were times during the next few weeks, when he almost wished it had been. From the moment the great wave picked him up, he remembered nothing until he regained consciousness to find himself in his bunk, but the others told him that he too had been washed over the side and then, more fortunate, than the mate, back again. Swept along the deck by the sea, he had been dashed against some fitting and on being picked up, blood was pumping out of a wound, near his left temple. He was carried down the cabin steps and put into his bunk and it was only then, found that the wound in his head was by no means the worst of his injuries; it was, indeed, only a superficial one, much less serious than the amount of blood would suggest. The right thigh had been broken, well up, and the journey from the deck to his bunk had made the break much worse, so that one end of the broken bone was actually sticking out of the flesh. In addition, some ribs on the right side had been broken and both arms were injured.

The sea that had swept the mate overboard and done its best to kill Captain Murray, had made a clean sweep of the decks. The binnacle was swept overboard, together with the big mainsail which it had been intended to bend on, also a two-ton water tank lashed to the bulwarks. To add to the confusion, some ninety-gallon drums of fuel oil lashed on deck, had broken adrift and were crashing about from side to side, and threatening to go through the bulwarks. As regards saving the mate, who had been swept overboard, Mr. Munn remarked: "To have put out a boat would have been impossible, nor would it have lived a moment if we had done so". He goes on to say that by six o'clock that night, a tremendous sea was running which the vessel rode out under a close-reefed mainsail and trysail.

There then commenced for Captain Murray a period of extreme anguish, with no possibility of relief. Seamen are mostly optimists and along with the other stores handed over to the trading post at Ponds Inlet, practically the entire contents of the medicine chest had been left behind, so that there was nothing to relieve the pain of his injuries. He recorded: "I lay there, for over five weeks before I could receive any medical aid, the vessel rolling and tossing about practically all the time. It took everyone all their time to look after themselves, without worrying about me".

The vessel herself was in a bad plight, short of fuel and food, the binnacle swept away, the chronometers run down and with the mate gone, no-one with any real knowledge of navigation. There was however, one man aboard with whose help Captain Murray was able to get some idea of the ship's position. This was Wilfred Caron, the young French Canadian, who was, incidentally, a nephew of Captain Bernier, famous French Canadian Arctic seafarer, whose name appears so often in the Arctic Pilot. While at Godhavn Captain Murray had rated his chronometers and had shown Wilfred Caron, how to take a sight. He knew how to bring the sun down, but could not read the vernier, so after the accident which nearly finished Captain Murray, he would take the sun at noon and the captain would work out the latitude. With the chronometers stopped there was no possibility of getting the longitude and all that could be done was to steer due east along a parallel of latitude. Very fortunately, an old compass card was found and a binnacle of sorts was rigged up, and although the compass error could only be guessed at, they were able to steer an approximate easterly course.

In spite of his injuries Captain Murray drove himself, to write up his log, only six days after the accident. On the 24th, they managed to signal the American wooden steamer *Afalky*, of Seattle and obtained from her some provisions and coal. The steamer sent out a radio message telling of the *Albert*'s plight and in response a destroyer was sent out to look for her, but failed to find her. About this time, Captain Murray recorded in his log:"I am having the most miserable time of my life. At times I felt it would have been better, had I been swept over with the mate, and at those moments I would tell myself to fight down such cowardly thoughts, for the sake of those at home. At that time they were 300 miles west and 90 miles south of Rockall, the lonely pinnacle out in the Atlantic, far to the west of Scotland, and were hoping to pick up Barra Head, southernmost point of the Hebrides, within a few days. But then they were struck by a SSE gale and on 2nd November, obtained their position, from a large Swedish full-rigged ship and found they were 300 miles north-west of Barra Head. Captain Murray's log recorded "Disagreeable weather, day after day, strong winds and dirty wet weather. We had only seen the sun four or five times, from the time I had the accident, until our arrival at Tobermory". On 5th November, they picked up the Barra Head light and anchored off Tobermory, Island of Mull, on 7th November. According to Mr. Munn, the *Albert*, was posted missing at Lloyds but this seems very doubtful. Despite her arduous voyage the *Albert*, had been only 37 days from Godhavn to Tobermory and a vessel would have to be very much more overdue than that, to be posted missing at Lloyds, and in addition, she had been reported by the *Afalky*, when 24 days out. Captain Murray closed his log with the words "End of voyage 1919, bad ending for me". He was taken ashore at Tobermory and when the doctors saw the state of his thigh, they marvelled that he could have survived. It seems certain, that few men could have done, with the two ends of the broken thigh bone, protruding from the flesh. These two ends had coagulated and a nob had formed on each, and before any attempt could be made to knit the broken parts together, these nobs had to be removed.

It was a long time before even Captain Murray could think of going back to sea. The long period during which the thigh had received no attention made a complete and satisfactory cure impossible and he was left with a bad limp. The summer of 1920, was spent at home in Wormit and of it he remarked: "it was the first summer I had spent at home for twenty years, but I can't say I enjoyed it, being in bed all the time".

After putting the captain ashore at Tobermory, the *Albert*, proceeded to Peterhead, by way of the Caledonian Canal, and as Mr. Munn said, "the disastrous voyage of 1919, was over". Masters with any Arctic experience were, by this time, a dying breed and when the *Albert*, left Peterhead, on June 21st 1920, she had a master with no experience of ice navigation and it was the elderly bosun, Booth, who had sailed in the ship on earlier voyages with Captain Murray, who proved of the greatest value. The *Albert* arrived at Ponds Inlet on September 2nd, and Mr. Munn left her there, to spend the winter in the Arctic, while the ketch went back to Peterhead with her cargo of furs and other produce. The different conditions aboard her with Captain Murray absent are illustrated by the following remark from Mr. Munn: "On September 15th, the most violent gale I had experienced in Ponds Inlet, blew from the south-east and next year I learnt that the bosun of the *Albert*, old Booth, on his own responsibility, ran the ketch back fifty miles, to make a shelter he knew of, where they rode it out with both anchors down. The captain was hors de combat, in his cabin and unable to give any orders".

CHAPTER TWELVE

AFTER THE GREAT WAR

THE Spring of 1921, eighteen months after the accident, found Captain Murray able to walk with a stick but still under the doctor, for the wound in his thigh obstinately refused to heal. For some men the accident aboard the *Albert* would have meant an end to any more seafaring, but not for Captain Murray. Letters had come from London asking when he would be able to take command of the *Albert* again and he tells us what he did. "I knew it was hopeless asking the doctor if I could go back to sea, so seeing I could get along with a stick, I packed up one day and went off without telling him I was going. We sailed for the Arctic from Peterhead on 22nd June 1921. A fortnight later, when we were in mid-Atlantic, I was bathing the wound in my thigh with lysol and water when I felt the wool catch on something, which appeared to be a piece of bone. I pulled at it and a piece of bone, almost as long as my little finger and as thick as the middle of it, came away. It was sharply pointed at both ends and there were two small holes in it, made by the screws of the plate which had been put into my thigh by the surgeon". The above is just one example, if it were needed, of the resolute character of John Murray, for to pull a piece of bone out of one's thigh without an anaesthetic must have been a painful business. Once rid of the splinter the wound healed rapidly.

The master of a vessel such as the *Albert*, which could only make headway, by constantly altering course through the open lanes in the ice, could not do his navigating from the deck but went up into the crow's nest and gave his orders for helm and engines from there. It is a further indication of the type of man he was that Captain Murray, already well over fifty and partly crippled, could get up aloft in that small ship, whose motion must have been wicked at times, and stay up there for hours at a time in the bitter cold.

The *Albert* arrived at Ponds Inlet on August 17th and Mr. Munn tells us that it was with "great joy" that he found Captain Murray again in command. In his book Mr. Munn gives us an example of how longevity can provide a link with events long past. He relates that during that winter of 1920/21 an old man was brought to see him from a point far away, in one of the deep bights opening off Eclipse Sound, the object of his visit being to "see the white man once more". Claiming to be "the oldest man in the world" he said he had seen an Arctic explorer (perhaps Sir John Ross) at Ponds Inlet in 1826 and could remember his ship. If his story was correct, he must have been close on one hundred years old. This would be all the more remarkable since Eskimos do not seem to be particularly long-lived.

From Ponds Inlet the *Albert* went south to another trading post of the company at Cumberland Gulf, Mr. Munn going in the vessel and leaving Wilfred Caron in charge at the inlet. From Cumberland Gulf the ketch made a good run home, arriving at Peterhead after a passage of 20 days. The next year, 1922, Mr. Munn decided to fit out the *Albert* at Halifax N.S. instead of in Scotland and left Peterhead on 3rd June, Captain Murray being still in command. The passage across the North Atlantic was a tedious one due to bad weather and engine trouble and the *Albert* was 40 days out when she arrived at Halifax. She left again on 19th July on what was to prove an eventful voyage. The season of 1922 turned out to be the worst for ice in Davis Straits for many years and all the way up to Cumberland Gulf the *Albert* had difficulty making any headway. On 1st August she was in the vicinity of Kekerten, where Munn's company had their station, and being unable to reach it went on to Ushuadloo, further north, where they were welcomed by the Eskimos and a great feast and dance was held. The Eskimo women provided the music on melodeons, together with an elderly Eskimo who played the fiddle and claimed Scottish nationality through having made a trip to Peterhead.

Later the *Albert* worked her way up to Ponds Inlet to her

station at Button Point, where she arrived on 27th August. Wilfred Caron, who had been left in charge, had a good cargo of Arctic produce for them, with a large quantity of whale oil. This had been obtained from a large Greenland whale killed by an Eskimo with one shot from a .303 rifle, a unique happening. It had been driven into shallow water by killer whales, those horrors of the sea, and in consequence could not escape. The shot had been fired into its side at close range and penetrated the heart. Mr. Munn remarked somewhat mournfully, " It yielded me 1600 lbs of bone and about 20 tons of oil. There had been a time in the '90's when whalebone was worth over £2000 a ton and the Dundee whaling ships were making money for their owners. I sold this bone for just over £500 per ton and thought I was lucky to get it. One of its uses still is to weave threads of it into the heaviest Mandarin silk, to stiffen it and make it stand out well". Mr. Munn does not tell us what he got for his whale oil, but it was probably about £20 a ton.

It was on this visit to Ponds Inlet that Captain Murray saw the Eskimo Nookudlah who had shot Janes, the white trader. He and the other two who were charged with being his accomplices, Oorooreungnak and Ahteetah, were there with Staff Sergeant Joy, who had made an epic journey to arrest them. It was an appropriate part of the whole bizarre story, that the three prisoners attended the festivities held aboard the *Albert* during her visit to Ponds Inlet and seemed unconcerned as to what might befall them. Only Nookudlah seemed despondent at times. The eyes are not always "the windows of the soul" and faces do not always show the real person behind them, but a photo of Nookudlah shows a very pleasant man with no look of a murderer about him.

From Ponds Inlet the *Albert* returned to Cumberland Gulf, the voyage being made more difficult through one of the passengers going temporarily insane. Mr. Munn wished to call at Cape Kater, about 250 miles north of the Cumberland Gulf, to leave some supplies with an Eskimo, Akko-molee, for whom he had a great regard, but the ice prevented them getting there and they had to miss it. At the entrance to Cumberland Gulf they found the Hudson Bay Company's steamer *Bayeskimo*, then on her maiden voyage, slowly making her way out. A

Hudson Bay Company's Inspector, Mr. Parsons, was on board and told them that the ship had been damaged in the ice and was leaking and that the captain, afraid of being beset, had abandoned the idea of going to the Company's station further up the Gulf. From this, there arose an incident referred to by the newspapers of the time, as an example of Aesop's Fable of the Lion and the Mouse. The *Albert* was asked if she would go up the Gulf and deliver the *Bayeskimo*'s stores to the Hudson Bay Company's station there, the steamer agreeing to take the passenger aboard the *Albert* who had temporarily lost his reason. Captain Murray, being quite confident he could get up the Gulf, agreed to the proposal and also took aboard some Ponds Inlet Eskimos who were going further up the Gulf. The *Bayeskimo* was a powerful vessel of 1391 gross tons and 212 feet long, compared with the *Albert*'s 155 tons and length of 100 feet, and yet the little vessel, backed by Captain Murray's nearly forty years of Arctic experience, was able to work her way through the ice, in a manner quite beyond the big powerful steamer.

Mr. Munn's station in the Gulf was at Kekerten, situated among a group of islands lying athwart it, and the *Albert* arrived there without much difficulty. Kekerten, incidentally, appears to be a variation of the Eskimo word "kekertang", meaning island, and there is another group in Franklin Strait, far to the north-west, known to the natives as the Kiker-ton Islands. Having arrived at Kekerten the *Albert* found what Mr. Munn made no bones about calling "an unpleasant surprise",—he was faced with having to take a shipwrecked crew back to the U.K. in the tiny *Albert*: the *Albert* was only one of three Scottish vessels which made trading voyages to the Arctic this year, the others being the auxiliary three-masted schooner *Easonian*–Captain J. C. Taylor, owned by the Cumberland Gulf Trading Company of Dundee, and the auxiliary two-masted schooner *Vera*–Captain John Pearson, whose owners were the Sabellum Trading Company of London. The *Vera*, of only 97 tons gross, built back in 1876 as the yacht *Oneagh*, was badly damaged by ice in Davis Straits and being unable to reach her trading posts made for Holstenborg, in Greenland, to effect repairs before proceeding with the voyage.

There, while beached to carry out the repairs, she fell over on her side and filled on the rising tide, becoming a total loss. Captain Pearson was a very experienced seaman, having gone to sea as an apprentice in the wooden barque *Earl Dalhousie*, carrying emigrants to Australia, in 1879. Later he served in the whaler *Arctic* to finish his apprenticeship and was subsequently mate of the well-known whaler *Terra Nova*. In the '90's he was for some years, master of the Dundee barque *Glenogle*. His life story appears in my book "Four Captains", Brown, Son & Ferguson Ltd., 1975. The *Easonian* was a very smart little vessel, built in 1918 at Pasages, Spain, as the *Nuestra Senora de Arantzazu* and registered in Bilbao until brought under the British flag. Another Spanish sailing vessel, built about the same time which was almost a sister ship and had a similar type of name, was the *Nuestra Senora de Arritoquieta*. The *Easonian* had already done a season in the Arctic under Captain Taylor when she set out from Dundee on 17th June 1922 bound for Cumberland Gulf. Captain Taylor also had had experience of the Arctic, having served his apprenticeship in the whalers *Active*, *Morning* and *Scotia* and sailed as an officer in the *Morning*. His two mates, Burnett and Morrison, were both of them men with sail experience. The *Easonian's* auxiliary was a semi-diesel Kromaut which gave a lot of trouble and kept her in port long after she should have sailed for the Arctic. The voyage out to Davis Straits was made mostly under sail because of the defective engine and there were occasions when to help the ship along, the crew resorted to the back-breaking expedient of towing her with a boat. Having reached Davis Straits, Captain Taylor put into Holstenborg to repair a propeller clutch. Leaving there three days later, she reached her first trading post, Blacklead Island, where she got ashore while approaching the settlement. Refloated undamaged, she later went up to Bon Accord, at the head of the Gulf, where 75 white whales were killed. Of this part of the Gulf, the "Arctic Pilot, Vol. III" says: "The whole of this coast is dangerous on account of the scattered numerous rocks in the entrances to the fiords and the strong currents".

At Bon Accord, disaster overtook the *Easonian* when the flywheel of the engine flew off and smashed itself to pieces.

After that, she was a sailing vessel only and it was decided to beach her at Kekerten and remove the propeller so that it would not hinder her sailing qualities for the voyage home. And it was at Kekerten that the final disaster occurred, when she got on fire and burned herself right down to the water's edge, the fire being started by the sparking plugs in the lighting set. The only good thing about the destruction of this fine little ship was that no-one was hurt. The date of the fire was 8th September 1922.

The prospects for the crew of the *Easonian* were now grim, for with winter imminent, the entire crew, ten in number, were left literally in the clothes they stood up in; and as a photograph of them with the burned-out shell of their ship as a background shows, they were wearing European clothes, unthinkable as a dress for an Arctic winter. Their one hope was that the *Bayeskimo* might call and a lookout was kept for her from a nearby hill, although no-one had much hope of being rescued and after a few days all hands were measured for winter clothing, to be made by the Eskimo women. Unknown to the *Easonian*'s crew, the *Bayeskimo* was unable to reach them and it was the little *Albert* which rescued them from a winter in the Arctic. The stranded crew of the burned-out schooner were in an Eskimo igloo one night when one of the Eskimos raised his hand and said: "Ship coming", and as if to confirm what he said, all the dogs in the settlement started barking. Everyone rushed out and there were the lights of a ship—the *Albert*. She continued up the Gulf to deliver the *Bayeskimo*'s cargo and then returned to pick up the *Easonian*'s men. After making a call at Blacklead Island, the ketch set off for home on what was to be a very trying passage. Only ten hours after leaving Blacklead Island the engine failed completely and from then on the *Albert* was a sailing vessel.

Across the mouth of Cumberland Gulf the ice was impenetrable for an engineless vessel and Captain Murray at once gave the ketch a good offing from the floe edge. It was fortunate that he did so, as for three days it blew a gale and without that offing the *Albert* would certainly have ended her career crushed by the great floes. After the gale Captain Murray spent many hours up in the crow's nest working the vessel, under sail alone, through the pack ice into open water. From then on she had variable weather across the Atlantic and arrived at Peterhead on 25th October, 43 days after leaving Blacklead Island. Things were not easy with such a crowd of people aboard that tiny vessel and the remark of one of the crew of the *Easonian* that they "had to put up with considerable inconvenience on the trip to Peterhead" was probably an understatement. It was perhaps fortunate that in the words of Mr. Munn when speaking of this passage, "as well as being a fine seaman, Murray is a very fine character".

"ALBERT REVILLON" with topmasts shortened

This 1922 voyage of the *Albert* was her last for Mr. Munn and Captain Murray, for the former shortly afterwards sold his stations to the Hudson's Bay Company. The *Albert* was handed over with the rest of the company's assets and soon afterwards stranded near Lossiemouth. She was refloated and later came under the Danish flag, being registered at Trangiavaag, in the Faeroe Islands, and the last Captain Murray heard of his old ship was of her having been seen in St. John's, NFL.

Schr "Albert Revillon"
Loading boats for Hudson Bay

Captain Murray was now 56 and in the Spring of 1924 went out to Liverpool N.S. and joined the three-masted schooner *Albert Revillon*, owned by the well-known Arctic trading company of Revillon Freres. She was one of the large number of schooners built in the British North America during and after the First Great War and had been built at Littlebrook, N.S. in 1920 as the *Maxwell C*. When Captain Murray joined her, she was having an auxiliary motor fitted. In this ship he had a Newfoundlander named Parsons as mate and Parsons' son as a second mate. The years from 1923 to 1926 were spent in serving the Revillon Company's trading posts in the Arctic and Captain Murray had very little to say about this period. He mentioned having carried on one occasion an ornithologist called Dr. Sutton who claimed to be the inventor of the tracer bullet. Dr. Sutton was going north to find the breeding place of the grey goose and discovered it far up on the east side of Foxe Channel.

Revillon Freres had another schooner, the *Jean Revillon*, and in 1927 they were sold to the Hudson's Bay Company, the *Albert Revillon* becoming the *Fort Garry* and the *Jean Revillon* the *Fort James*. Captain Murray remained in the ship after the transfer, thus returning to the employ of the company he had first served back in 1891, when he had made the eventful trip to York Factory as an A.B. in the old *Perseverance*. He had later commanded the barque under Hudson's Bay Company's ownership. On 1st June 1927, he left St. John's NFL for the north and later that summer a tribute to his skill as an Arctic navigator was paid by Mr. Parsons, the Hudson's Bay Company's Fur Commissioner who, broadcasting from the s.s. *Nascopie* said: "The *Fort Garry* has set off for Ponds Inlet and if anyone can get her there, Captain Murray can". He spoke from experience, for it was he who had been aboard the *Bayeskimo* when she was unable to get into Cumberland Gulf in 1922 and the *Albert* had delivered her cargo for her. The *Fort Garry* had never been as far north as Ponds Inlet before.

By 1928 the *Fort Garry* and the *Fort James* were fitted with refrigerating machinery and Captain Murray did a season at Lewisport, NFL in charge of the two vessels during the salmon fishing season. They brought salmon from various points on the Newfoundland coast to Lewisport, where the fish were put aboard freight trains to be taken to St. John's.

It was in 1928 that Captain Murray had his first command in a full powered steamer, the Hudson's Bay Company's *Nascopie*. This vessel had been built in Newcastle in 1912 for the well-known Newfoundland firm of Job Brothers and was acquired by the Hudson Bay Company in 1915. Major W. H. Green's book "The Wooden Walls Among the Ice Floes" mentions that the *Nascopie* made no sealing voyages between 1916 and 1926 and "very few after that", but in Captain Murray's time in her, he made an annual voyage out of St. John's. He was no stranger to the sealing, having been there in the *Esquimaux* in 1890, nearly forty years earlier, but had the very well-known Captain Abram Kean as a sealing master. Captain Kean had been born in Newfoundland in 1855 so was nearly 75, when aboard the *Nascopie* and was approaching his target of one million seals. He wrote a book about his life called "Old and Young Ahead" and in it refers to the *Nascopie* as "one of the most powerful ice-breakers in the sealing fleet". Between 1898 and 1934 he was sealing master of the following ships: *Aurora, Terra Nova, Florizel, Stephano,* among others. He reached his target of one million seals in 1934 in the steamer *Beothic*, owned by Bowring Brothers, when he was 79 years old, and received the O.B.E. from King George V to mark the achievement. The *Nascopie* had her decks sheathed with wood to protect them from the "sparables" (spiked boots) of the "sweilers" (sealers) who lived in the 'tween-decks under what must have been more comfortable conditions than they had aboard such vessels as the *Esquimaux*. There were five master watchers, each in charge of a group which would spread out on the ice from the ship for their butcher's work. Captain Murray remarked that they were very dirty and unkempt by the end of the trip and one would never recognise them once they had been cleaned up.

After the sealing the *Nascopie* went up to Davis Straits and Hudson Bay with cargo and passengers for the Company's posts there, going as far north as Lancaster Sound, in 74° north. In addition to wireless the *Nascopie* was fitted with a gyro compass, that most valuable aid to navigation in the

CAPTAIN MURRAY on bridge of "NASCOPIE"

Arctic, where the proximity of the magnetic pole, makes the magnetic compass so sluggish as to be nearly useless. The echo-sounder and radar were still to come, but even without those fittings, standard today, Captain Murray must have often looked back at his days in the old *Perseverance* and the brig *Alert* and the other windships he had sailed in, and marvelled at the changes he had seen.

The *Nascopie* laid-up every winter in Ardrossan, which was a very suitable arrangement for Captain Murray, with a wife and family in Wormit, but 1930 saw the end of his time in her and he was at home throughout 1931. Then in 1932 he returned to the service of the Hudson's Bay Company in a very different type of ship in a very different locality. Going out to Vancouver overland, he joined the small wooden motor-vessel *Karise*, which had been chartered by the company, taking out with him a former Brixham fisherman, Summers by name, as mate and a man called Knightly as second mate.

The *Karise* was a vessel of 542 gross tons built at Thuro, Denmark, in 1918 as the *Svendborgsund* and fitted with one of those early diesels which were an engineer's nightmare. In this ship Captain Murray made a voyage right up past Point Barrow, in 71° north, on the very roof of the world, to the Coppermine River and back to Seattle. It was not an easy voyage for any ship and was made very much more difficult for the *Karise* by the fact that the engine gave constant trouble. Captain Murray joined her on 22nd June 1932, left Vancouver on 30th June and within a day or so of leaving was a salvage job, a bottom-end bearing being burned out 30 miles south of Alert Harbour, on the north coast of Vancouver Island. Fore-and-aft sails were hoisted and later the tug *Leadwell* towed them into Alert Harbour for 200 dollars. Leaving again on 6th July the *Karise* arrived at Dutch Harbour, in the Aleutians, on 18th July and after taking on bunker oil left again on the 20th. The log records, that the vessel was leaking while there. On the 28th she left Wainwright, Alaska, for Point Barrow and the log contains the following entry: "Afraid to stop our engines, no air to start it again as a compressor out of commission". Throughout the log there are constant references to engine breakdowns. On the 29th July: "Passeng-

ers left ship as she was having engine trouble, and went by
motor-boat to Point Barrow". It took two days to repair the
engines that time and they got under way again on 1st August
and went to Point Barrow. There Captain Murray was asked if
he could do anything about salvaging cargo from the Hudson's
Bay Company's steamer, *Baychimo*, abandoned near Point
Barrow. The log tells us that he took on board 14 bales of furs
salvaged from the *Baychimo* and engaged six Eskimos at a
wage of $65 plus a bonus of $10 to work cargo.

Leaving Point Barrow on 1st August the log records on the
3rd: "Engineer lay down for a rest after 18 hours work". In
various ways the *Karise* was a badly designed vessel. For
example, the whistle was operated by compressed air and if it
was blown, then the main engine stopped! The windlass was
worked by means of a long shaft which also drove the winches
and as the power to drive it was also compressed air, both
could not be used at the same time. Much of the cargo had to
be loaded and discharged by hand. On 5th August, at Herschel
Island, in the Yukon, the Royal Canadian Mounted Police
vessel *St. Roch* was there with them and towed the *Karise* off
the jetty when her engines once again refused to work.
Leaving Herschel Island there were ten passengers aboard the
tiny vessel, including a Bishop Geddes and a Reverend Morris.
On 11th August "the wireless dynamo burst into flames" but
the fire was put out in less than two minutes. On 12th August
at Pierce Point: "Tried to pick up our motor-boat, our engine
not working satisfactorily but afraid to stop as we would
probably have difficulty starting again". On 14th August there
was trouble of another sort: "Compass very unsatisfactory".
15th August: "Sent all hands on shore to load the schooner
Aklavik for Reid Island. Had a visit from Patsy Klinkenberg and
Ike Bolt. *St. Roch* arrived and had a visit from Inspector
Eames". 17th August: "Arrived at Coppermine River" and
while the *Karise* was there, a seaplane arrived to take off some
of the furs salvaged from the *Baychimo*. The use of an
aeroplane to load furs, lays emphasis on the changes which
had taken place since Captain Murray first went to sea in
1884, 48 years earlier. The heavier-than-air flying machine
was still a dream at that time. On the 25th August, they left the

"KARISE" ex "SVENDBORGSUND"

Coppermine River with "a very assorted crowd of passengers aboard: R.C.M.P. Inspector Eames, Eskimos and their children and H.B.C. managers". On 28th August, the log recorded "Rolling very heavily, unable to have any food cooked". On 30th August, the *Karise* arrived back at Herschel Island and three days later, at Point Barrow, landed the Eskimos who had been engaged for cargo work. A week was spent at Dutch Harbour for engine repairs and the voyage ended at Seattle, on 27th September.

The log from which the above extracts were taken, gives no idea at all of the real dangers and hardships of the *Karise*'s voyage, and Captain Murray being what he was, a man of action rather than words, said nothing at all about the voyage. But an account given in the book "The Royal Canadian Mounted Police", of a voyage in the *St. Roch*, in the same area in 1935, gives a very good picture of what conditions were like, and there is no reason to suppose that they were any worse then than Captain Murray had in 1932. The *St. Roch*, specially constructed for ice work and rigged as a two-masted bald-headed schooner, with a 150 H.P. diesel engine, left Dutch Harbour, in July 1935, bound for R.C.M.P., posts along the Arctic coastline of the Yukon, among them Herschel Island, Coppermine and Pierce Point, all of which were visited by Captain Murray in the *Karise*. The *St. Roch*, slowly fought her way eastwards through the ice, sometimes using blasting powder to clear the way, until at the Demarcation Point, between American Alaska and the Canadian Yukon, she was jammed so badly that her crew hurriedly packed their gear ready to abandon her. Then, after drifting helplessly backwards and forwards in the ice, they received a call for help from the schooner *Fort James*, (previously mentioned as having been employed at the salmon fishing out of Lewisport, NFL), which had smashed her rudder and propeller in the ice. The *St. Roch*, managed to get to the damaged ship and later both of them were jammed in the ice together. It was lucky the *St. Roch*, was there, for suddenly the *Fort James*, heeled right over and sank. According to the writer of the account, the *Fort James* was a sister ship to the famous Nova Scotian fishing schooner *Bluenose*, which had been designed and built to win for Nova

Scotia the annual race for deep sea fishing schooners and did so several times. The *Bluenose*, was a famous little ship whose name will certainly be long remembered in Nova Scotia, but she was built as a fisherman and not primarily for work in the ice and had comparatively fine lines with a deep keel. So constructed, the *Fort James* could not ride over the ice as the *St. Roch* could do, and it was her deep keel which finished her, for it was torn right off and she quickly filled. There was just time to grab two Eskimo women and six children and shoot some Eskimo dogs, to save them from drowning before the schooner sank. She was long survived by the *Bluenose*, which came to her end in January 1946, not in the cold waters of Nova Scotia, but on a reef off the coast of Haiti, being then 25 years old.

The voyage in the *Karise*, brought Captain Murray's sea career to an end. He was now in his 65th year and retired to his home at Wormit, just below the Tay Bridge. In 1935, he met again the Mr. R. G. Flaherty, whom he had first encountered in Hudson Bay in 1914, when Flaherty was in the schooner *Laddie*, and who was now a prominent film director. As a result of this meeting Captain Murray went over to the Arran Islands, off the west coast of Eire, to give technical advice in the harpooning of sharks, this being required for the film "Man of Arran". He stayed there for several months and harpooned about ten sharks, the longest of them 29 feet, playing a part as a stand-in for a professional actor.

Captain Murray lived in Wormit for the rest of his life, dying there in 1950, when he was 82. He was the last of the old-time whaling masters.

ADDITIONAL NOTES

STAFF SERGEANT Joy, the man who arrested Nookudlah in 1921, came from Bedford, England. He was eventually promoted to Inspector, and in April 1932, died of congestion of the lungs while still a young man.

The Inspector Eames, whom Captain Murray met while he was in the *Karise*, was earlier concerned in a case which is outstanding even in R.C.M.P. annals. In 1931, a man called Johnson arrived in the Fort McPherson district of the North West Territory and quickly aroused the suspicions of the police by his violent behaviour, towards Indian trappers and others. Two policemen were sent to investigate and were met with rifle fire which wounded one of them. Later Johnson shot dead another policeman, and before he was finally killed by a police bullet yet another man, a soldier, had been badly wounded. Johnson's identity was apparently never discovered but he was thought to be an American criminal who had entered Canadian territory to escape the law in his own country.

Captain Murray always spoke very highly of the Eskimos and throughout his life among them, never mentioned drunkenness or violence towards white men. But one gets a rather different picture of Eskimos from the book "Fifty Years Below Zero", by C.D. Brower. There he tells us that the Eskimos at Cape Prince of Wales, Alaska, bore an "unsavoury reputation", among whalers, several of whom were killed by them, at different times. But one suspects that in their case bad treatment by white men and the sale to them of whisky had something to do with conduct which seems quite out of line with the Eskimo character.

No book about the Scottish whalers can omit mention of Captain Andrew Yule, of Dundee. Born in 1835, he was in command of a Montrose brig, the *Gazelle*, in 1863, when he

168

was only 28. In his next ship, the *Isabella*, he took a cargo of timber to Dundee, which was used to build the *Esquimaux*. He was given the command of her when completed and made his first whaling voyage in her in 1866, retaining the command until 1879. Leaving the sea in 1883, he became Harbourmaster of Dundee, and occupied this position until 1920, when he was 85 years old. He died in 1935, at the age of 100.

Captain William Fraser Milne, who had the *Albert* before Captain Murray, was born at Peterhead in 1851, and spent most of his sea life in whalers. His first ship was the old *Perseverance*, and later he was in the *Esquimaux*, with Captain Yule and had this ship as his first command in 1883. In 1890, he took the *Maud*, a barque built at Whitby in 1865, and converted into an auxiliary by Captain William Adams in 1884. He lost her in 1892, being wrecked in the ice near Coutts Inlet, south of Ponds Inlet, in 72 north. When lost she was the best fished ship that season. The crew was rescued by the whaler/sealer *Eagle*, of St. John's NFL. In 1893, he went in the *Eclipse*, and had her until 1907 and his last whaler was the *Diana*, another of the auxiliary barques, built at Drammen, Norway, in 1872. When the whaling was finished he commanded steamers until his retirement, and died just before World War II.

Svend Foyn, the man who revolutionised the business of whale catching, was born at Tonsberg in 1809. His father, a shipmaster, died when he was a child and he went to sea when only eleven. He seems to have been a mixture of godliness, tenacity and business acumen and all his life had a great belief in God's personal interest in himself. At an early age he was in command of an old full-rigged ship called the *Familien*, owned by his mother and elder brother and in this vessel used to go round the more remote fjords, supplying the communities there with goods they could not otherwise have obtained. To navigate a beamy old square-rigger in those narrow precipitous fjords, where the direction of the wind would at times be quite unpredictable, must have called for fine seamanship. Married at thirty to a clergyman's daughter,

"ECLIPSE"

the couple parted, amicably after only three years, leaving Svend Foyn, to devote himself entirely to work. He became interested in the possibilities of the Arctic in the 1840's, and sent a brig called the *Haabet* ("HOPE"), up north after seals. The trip was a failure, but he persisted, and on a subsequent voyage the brig came back with a load of 6,000 seals, which he sold at a good profit. Svend Foyn, was one of the founders of the Norwegian sealing industry, in the Arctic.

In 1863, Foyn had the schooner-rigged steamer *Spes et Fides* ("HOPE and FAITH"), built for him at Christiania and fitted her with the harpoon guns with which he had been experimenting for some time. The first cruise after finner whales, in 1864, was nearly Svend Foyn's last, for when firing his first harpoon, his foot was caught in a turn of the line and he was whisked overboard. Although now a man of fifty-five, he managed to free himself and got back aboard. On a later occasion the *Spes et Fides* was towed by a finner whale for twelve hours at a speed estimated by Svend Foyn at 18 knots. By that time, despairing of the whale ever becoming exhausted, the crew had to cut the tow-rope. The first few years of the *Spes et Fides* were not successful but in 1868, she came back from the Arctic having killed thirty finner whales, and it is usual to date modern whaling from that year. In 1870, Svend Foyn patented his harpoon gun, having been greatly assisted in finding a suitable explosive by a clergyman, Pastor Hans Morten Thrane Esmark, who had what some might think, a strange hobby for a priest of the church, the study of pyrotechnics and explosive chemistry.

There is little sentiment in business and despite the fact that as the prototype of the modern whale-catcher the *Spes et Fides* put Norway in the forefront of the whaling industry, no-one thought her worth preserving. She disappeared into complete obscurity, but there is evidence that she was still in service shortly before World War I, although not under her original name. She is not in "Lloyd's Register" for 1889/90, although there was at that time in the Register, a Norwegian brig called the *Spes & Fides*, built at Christiania, in 1865 and owned in Tonsberg, the great whaling port. Svend Foyn, died in 1894, aged 85, leaving behind him a name to be forever associated with whaling.

Captain Murray's *Balaena*, had a namesake under the American flag, an auxiliary barque of 524 tons gross, built in San Francisco, in 1883. A point of interest about this vessel is that she was built by Dickie Brothers, a company which had been founded by a Scot, who came from Tayport, Fife, where his family had a shipyard. Dickie Brothers built several other whalers besides the *Balaena*, including the *Bowhead, Orca* and *Narwhal*. Of these four ships the *Narwhal*, was the only one to survive, the other three all being lost in the Arctic. *Balaena*, was wrecked in 1901.

The risky nature of the sealers' and whalers' calling is very clearly illustrated in the book "The Wooden Walls Among the Ice Floes", by Major W.H. Greene. In that book a list is given of 58 "wooden walls", which were employed in the sealing out of St. John's, with their ending. Of the 58, 44 were lost, either when sealing or whaling, the usual epitaph being "lost while sealing", or "lost on rocks in a snowstorm", or "crushed by ice", or some such mournful phrase. And yet, by comparison, it could be claimed that in the area most used by Captain Murray, Hudson Strait and Hudson's Bay, navigational hazards were even greater than on the sealing grounds of Newfoundland. Perhaps the fogs which are the bane of the Newfoundland Banks, are not so bad, but the dangers from ice were undoubtedly greater, due to being so much further north; and where the waters round Newfoundland, were well charted Hudson's Bay, is not completely surveyed, even today. Also, the magnetic compass is practically useless in the entire area, Captain Murray knew so well. In spite of all this, Captain Murray, never lost a ship, in all his years in the north. Perhaps it was at least partly due to that "uncanny sense of ice navigation", referred to by H.T. Munn.

Captain Murray, came from Peterhead and mention was made at the start of this book, that there must be few people there who could not find seafarers, among their forebears. Captain Andrew Shewan, author of the book, "The Great Days of Sail", has something to say on this subject and about the men who went in the whalers. Himself a native of Peterhead, Captain Shewan's grandfather, was master of a whaler, who died as a result of hardships endured, when his ship was nipped in the ice in 1830, which was, incidentally, the most disastrous year in the whole history of British Whaling. Of 91 ships in Davis Straits, 19 were lost, 21 returned "clean", (not having caught a single fish), and many others were badly damaged. Captain Shewan's father was master of a schooner in the North Atlantic fish trade, when he was only 21, and later commanded the tea clippers *Lammermuir* and *Norman Court*. Captain Shewan went to sea in 1860, in the tea clipper *Chaa-Sze*, with his father.

He tells us that "the preponderance of Scottish skippers, in the China Clippers of the day, is to be noted", and mentions Reid of the *Wynaud*, Shewan of the *Lammermuir* and Jenkins of the *Warrior Queen*, as all coming from Peterhead. In the *Chaa-Sze*, they shipped a crowd of young fellows who had just paid-off a whaler, and were talked into joining a "south spainer", by the assurance that they would be back home in time for the 1861 whaling season. The mates had been warned by the master, Captain Shewan Senior, of the wild character of the "Greenlanders", for he knew they were "little versed in the niceties of sea discipline and apt to consider that 'Jack was as good as his master!'" It took both tact and firmness to get them to conform and to address the officers as "sir". Captain Shewan remarks that the ships they sailed in and the conditions under which they worked, made the whalemen entirely different to other classes of seafarers and they had about them "a freedom and a truculence of demeanour not often encountered on board the clippers". Long ocean passages in fine weather, they did not care for, and on such traverses were "by no means easy to manage", but it was in moments of crisis, that they showed up best, as when the *Chaa-Sze*, was dismasted, in the China Sea. The excitement and the danger seemed to stir their blood and they went about the job of getting things to rights with energy and cheerfulness. Captain Shewan remarks somewhat mournfully, that although Peterhead, was at its most prosperous when he was a boy, it continuously declined after that, 32 ships leaving for Greenland in 1860, but only a few by the 1870's.

THE "MAZINTHIEN"

MENTION of the *Mazinthien* is to be found in the book "My Naval Career and Travels" by Admiral E. H. Seymour. In 1867, Commander Seymour, as he then was, made a voyage to the Arctic in the *Mazinthien* to fill in time during a period when he was on half-pay. He tells us that her name was that of an Indian Chief, she having been built at Miramichi, New Brunswick, in 1850 as a merchant ship and made into a whaler almost immediately. Ship-rigged and engineless at first, she had engines put into her before Seymour sailed in her. Her captain while he was in her, was John Gray (2) "a first rate seaman and of a regular old whaling family". John Gray was a grandson of Captain David Gray, who had an earlier *Perseverance* out of Peterhead back in 1811. Of the family Basil Lubbock says: "The Grays of Peterhead have the distinction of being longer connected with the Arctic whaling than any other family in the British Isles, and the success of Peterhead whaling and sealing was due in a great degree to the Grays and their relatives". Captain John Gray (2) had the *Mazinthien* from 1862 to 1872, having previously had the *Queen* for ten years.

We are told that the crew of the *Mazinthien* was not "over sober" when they sailed and even the mate had imbibed rather freely, apparently to offset his anger at having found his fourteen-year-old son a stowaway on board. When the Commander sailed in her, the *Mazinthien* had a complement of 55 (as a merchant ship she would have had about 12). "She carried two mates, a spectioneer, four harpooners, two engineers and various other odd ratings, besides a surgeon". What he had to say about the surgeons would not please some of them, one fears: "These latter in the whaling ships were usually young medical students from Edinburgh, who having 'outrun the constables' felt safer at sea, and not anxious to revisit 'Auld Reekie' till they had a few bawbees in their pocket". One can readily think of one whaler surgeon at least who did not fit into this category, and that was Conan Doyle, creater of Sherlock Holmes, who made a voyage in 1880 as a surgeon of the *Hope*, the ship of which Captain Murray was second mate in 1892. Charles Edward Smith, too, surgeon of the whale-ship *Diana* of Hull on her ill-rated voyage of 1866/67 was no young spark on the run from the "constables", as his diary, contained in the book "From the Deep of the Sea" shows.

Admiral Seymour tells us that "the dirt of a whaler must almost be seen to be believed; as for the men, their faces become like niggers, and washing at all with many is relegated to a very dubious date". As a boy the mate of the *Mazinthien* had been in the whaler *Enterprise* with Captain Martin in 1845 when they had met Sir John Franklin's ships, the *Erebus* and *Terror*, in Melville Bay and told Seymour something of the meeting. As related in the book, the *Enterprise* was the last vessel to see the *Erebus* and *Terror* but it is generally stated that the whaler *Prince of Wales* of Hull was the last, on 26th July 1845. After that nothing more was heard of the two ships, for they were frozen-in north-west of King William's Land and their crews perished to a man after abandoning the ships when their food was exhausted and they tried to reach Hudson's Bay.

Sunday was just like any other day aboard the whalers and Admiral Seymour tells us that there was a similarity between them and a certain West African palm-oil trader he knew of. Passing Cape Palmas outward-bound the captain produced a board with the word "Sunday" chalked on it, threw it over the side and told the crew: "No more Sundays, boys, until we pass this point going north!"

1867 was a bad year for whaling and the *Mazinthien*, like several other ships that year, did not get a single "fish", although Seymour remarks that owing to the large number of seals killed the voyage paid the owners "very well" (at this time seal oil was worth about £40 a ton). In 1866, also, the *Mazinthien* had returned home "clean". The author concluded his chapter on the *Mazinthien* by telling us that the crew of the ship were "as fine a set of honest hardy seamen as one could find". Captain John Gray left the *Mazinthien* in 1872 and from 1873 until 1891 had the *Hope (2)* which had been built for him by Hall of Aberdeen in 1873. In 1891 the *Hope* was sold to Newfoundland owners, although registered in Greenock, and went to the sealing every year until wrecked at Byron Cove, Gulf of St. Lawrence, on 31st March 1901. Captain John Gray died in 1892, only a year after retiring.

Whaling had long passed its zenith when Captain Murray went to sea but there seems to be no doubt that there was still big profits to be made from it in the '70's and even later. This is indicated by the fact that a whaler, the *Arctic*, was built by Alexander Stephen at Dundee in 1875, and the whalers were very costly vessels to build because of the strength required to be able to contend with the ice. There was, too, an attempt made to add a vessel to the Dundee fleet by the purchase of a foreign whaler, but this ended in tragedy. A newspaper of 24th February 1877, reported that on 6th January the steamer *Spitzbergen* left Christiansand (Norway) for Dundee, having been purchased by Mr. Yeaman, M.P. from the Hamburg Polar Fishing Company. She had been fitted out at Christiansand and the newspaper recorded that "the passage would normally occupy not more than six days. Six weeks have now elapsed and nothing has been heard of the *Spitzbergen*. It is feared she went down in the storm which prevailed in the second week of January". On 3rd March (1877) a newspaper report stated that "information has been received at Dundee of the loss of the whaler *Spitzbergen* with all hands. The vessel belonged to a number of gentlemen who purchased her from the Hamburg Polar Fishing Company. She left Christiansand for Dundee two months ago and her papers have been cast ashore near Bergen. Her crew, 22 in number, were all foreigners". At the present time the loss of a vessel and 22 lives would make headline news, but at that time so many ships went missing that such an event meant very little, as the following will show: "Missing ships, 1873/74: Besides all the known and described wrecks with their 2100 lives lost, 150 British ships disappeared, clean gone, wiped out like a grease spot, never heard of after leaving port, this in one year's records. And with the 150 missing ships, 2381 missing men".

The *Arctic* of 1875 was not, however, the last whaler built in the U.K., that rather mournful honour belonging to the auxiliary barque *Terra Nova*, built at Dundee by Alexander Stephen in 1884 for themselves. Long afterwards, in 1901, Dundee also built the famous *Discovery*, although she was not built as a whaler but as a polar exploration ship. "Lloyd's Register" for 1902, has as her first commander "R. F. Scott, R.N.," who lost his life on the way back from the South Pole in 1912. Later, when owned by the Hudson's Bay Company, her captain was Alex Gray, a son of Captain John Gray of the whaling family.

THE WHALERS CAPTAIN MURRAY SAILED IN
(all built of wood)

Name	Rig	Where built	When	Remarks
Windward	Aux. bk.	Peterhead	1860	Wrecked 25.6.07
Perseverance	Barque	Sunderland	1852	Missing from 22.10.01
Esquimaux	Aux. ship	Dundee	1865	Became a hulk in U.S.A.
Alert	Brig	Peterhead	1853	Wrecked 9.01
Hope	Aux. ship	Aberdeen	1873	Wrecked 31.3.01
Active	Aux. bk.	Peterhead	1852	Lost off Orkneys in 1916
Scotia	Aux. bk.	Drammen	1872	Lost by fire in 1916
Balaena	Aux. bk.	Drammen	1872	Became a salvage hulk at Liverpool

WINTERS SPENT IN THE ARCTIC BY CAPTAIN MURRAY

1885/1886   In the *Perseverance* at Cumberland Sound
1892/1893   In the *Perseverance* at Repulse Bay
1894/1895   In the *Perseverance* at Depot Island, Hudson Bay
1896/1897   In the *Perseverance* at Repulse Bay
1899/1900   At Southampton Island
1900/1901   At Southampton Island
1901/1902   At Southampton Island
1903/1904   In the *Ernest William* at Repulse Bay
1905/1906   In the *Ernest William* close to Winter Island
1912/1913   In the *Albert* at Repulse Bay

The Sea Career of Captain John Murray

26.7.68 . . . . .Date of Birth
1884 . . . .*Windward* as O.S.
1885/1886 . . . .*Perseverance* as O.S.
1886/1889 . . . . *Helenslea* as apprentice
1889 . . . . .s.s. *Cairngorm* as A.B.
1890 . . . . *Esquimaux* as A.B.
1890 . . . .*Alert* as bosun
1890/1891 . . . . .s.s. *Meredith* as A.B.
1891 . . . . s.s. *Esk* as A.B.
1891 . . . .*Perseverance* as A.B.
1892 . . . . *Hope* as 2nd mate
1892/1893 . . . .*Perseverance* as 2nd mate
1894/1895 . . . . *Perseverance* as 1st mate
1896/1897 . . . . *Perseverance* as master
1898 . . . . *Active* as 1st mate
1899/1902 . . . . At Southampton Island
1903/1904 . . . . At Southampton Island and in *Ernest William*
1905/1906 . . . .*Ernest William* as master
1907 . . . . *Scotia* as 1st mate
1908/1910 . . . . *Balaena* as master
1911 . . . . s.s. *Glenisla* as 1st mate
1912/1913 . . . . *Albert* as master
1914 . . . .*Active* as master
1915/1919 . . . .*Albert* as master
1921/1922 . . . .*Albert* as master
1923/1926 . . . . *Albert Revillon* as master
1927 . . . . *Fort Garry* ex *Albert Revillon* as master
1927/1928 . . . . .At Lewisporte NFL.
1928/1930 . . . . s.s. *Nascopie* as master
1932 . . . . s.s. *Karise* as master
1933 . . . . At Arran Islands for film "Men of Arran"

BIBLIOGRAPHY

"Cadet to Commodore" by A. B. Armitage

"Whalemen Adventurers" by W. J. Dakin

"From the Deep of the Sea" by C. E. Smith

"Arctic Pilot", Vol. III

"Golden Gate" by Felix Riesenberg, Jr.

"Voyages and Wanderings etc." by J. Inches Thomson

"A Short History of Nanaimo" by Patricia M. Johnson

"San Francisco Bay" by J. H. Kemble

"From the Forecastle to the Cabin" by Captain Samuel Samuels

"A Shipbuilding History" (Alexander Stephen & Sons)

"The Wooden Walls among the Ice Floes" by Major W. H. Greene

"The Arctic Whalers" by Basil Lubbock

"The Log of Bob Bartlett" by Captain Robert A. Bartlett

"Pursuing the Whale" by Captain John A. Cook

"The Story of a Labrador Doctor" by Sir Wilfred Grenfell

"The Romance of Commerce" by J. M. Oxley

"Giant Fishes, Whales and Dolphins" by J. R. Norman and F. C. Fraser

"Benjamin Bowring and His Descendants" by A. C. Wardle

"The Royal Canadian Mounted Police" by L. C. Douthwaite

"The Gateway to the Polynia" by J. C. Wells

"From Edinburgh to the Antarctic" by W. C. Burn Murdoch

"OLd and Young Ahead" by Captain Abram Kean

"A Voyage to the Arctic in the whaler *Aurora*" by David Moore Lindsay

"The Great Days of Sail" by Captain Andrew Shewan

"A Whaling Cruise to Baffin's Bay" by Commander A. H. Markham, R.N.

"Old Whaling Days" by Captain William Barron

"My Naval Career and Travels" by Admiral of the Fleet, E. H. Seymour, R.N.

"New London Whaling Captains" by B. L. Collins

"Fifty Years Below Zero" by C. D. Brower

INDEX

A

F

Y